Living with Less

Living with Less

how to downsize to 100 personal possessions

MARY LAMBERT

CICO BOOKS

LONDON NEW YORK

Published in 2013 by CICO Books
an imprint of Ryland Peters & Small Ltd
20-21 Jockey's Fields, London WC1R 4BW
519 Broadway, 5th Floor, New York, NY 10012

www.cicobooks.com

10 9 8 7 6 5 4 3 2 1

A CIP catalog record for this book is available
from the Library of Congress and the British Library.

ISBN: 978 1 908170 98 9   646.7

Printed in China

Editor: Marion Paull
Designer: Alison Fenton
Illustrator: Robyn Neild

For digital editions, visit
www.cicobooks.com/apps.php

Contents

Introduction

I have worked with clients for over 13 years now, helping them to declutter their homes, and have written several successful books on the subject. But when I worked out the synopsis for this book—*Living with Less, how to downsize to 100 personal possessions*—I thought to myself: Is this going to be too difficult for people to do? Can anyone really live with so few items? I had read on the internet about people attempting to live with 100 or even 10 personal items but was it really possible? I decided to take on the challenge myself as I wrote the book and you can follow my experiences in my personal blog that appears in every chapter.

One reason I wanted to write this book is that for some time I have been concerned with the rampant consumerism that seems to have overtaken our society. Every time we turn on the television or go to town we encounter advertising for a new product. We are constantly encouraged to spend money on purchases that we "must have," but do we really need them? When a new version of a computer, television, or smart phone becomes available, we can feel obliged to buy it, or at least an upgrade, despite the fact that the one we have functions perfectly well for our needs.

My other concern is debt. With a credit card, it is so easy to spend beyond our means. We no longer feel the need to save up for something; we want the instant gratification of buying it straightaway. In these tough financial times, many of us have resorted to using several different cards to juggle our debt burden.

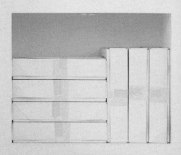
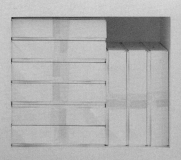

Changing attitudes

The only way to escape the debt spiral is to change your attitude to overspending. You will always have to buy food, clothes, and household items, of course, but you need to get out of the mindset of buying things just for the sake of it or to keep up with the neighbors. Isn't it better to try living a simpler, more minimalist lifestyle that can be more fulfilling than to carry on spending? This is where the idea of the 100-items challenge came in. The challenge is to pare down your personal belongings to just 100 items (you can group some things together as one) and live with just these for a year. You can replace items but you can't add to your list, unless you have managed to keep it to fewer than 100 to begin with. This is a difficult goal to achieve, especially if you love new clothes, but it will change your attitude to buying forever. It will also make you realize how you have been wasting your hard-earned money on things that you don't really need. All the money you save can go toward getting back on a firm financial footing and enjoying your preferred leisure pursuits.

Clothes make up 70 percent of the 100-item challenge but do you realize that most of us wear only 20 percent of these? The rest just hang in the closet. Selling or giving away the ones that you don't wear, that don't fit, or that you don't like any more will make you much more conscious of the outfits that flatter you. And you will become adept at mixing and matching the clothes you have left.

To help you cope with the challenge, I have split it down into achievable goals that you can work on over a period of a year (or longer if you need it). The clothes goal is the biggest one, so it has the longest time allocated to it—4½ months. Others deal with fewer items, such as your electrical, electronic, and sports equipment, so these are given just 1½ months each. Releasing these possessions from your life may be hard at first but it will make you feel so free and give you extra energy to try new activities.

Another benefit of letting go is that you can make money from selling those things. If you decide to donate some of your unwanted possessions to a good cause, such as a charity, instead, you will benefit from the "feel-good" factor.

Room by room

Just letting go of some of your personal possessions is not enough if you really want to live a simpler, less consumer-orientated life; you also need to appraise the household paraphernalia that you have accumulated over the years. If you look through each room in your home, you will notice how cluttered some areas have become, especially if you have been living there a while. Some rooms may be so full of furniture or equipment that you just don't use them any more. With my guidance you can allocate a certain number of hours to decluttering each room. Start on your worst room first, going through the main problem areas, using my solutions to help you restore some order to these over-loaded spaces.

A new life

As the energy shifts and changes in your home, your own perspective will change as well. You will start to enjoy the clearer and more functional spaces in all your rooms. By clearing out, you will also allow "space" in your mind for new creativity. You will no longer have to work so hard, because those tempting impulse buys will lose their appeal, and you will acquire a much more focused and honest approach to managing all of your finances.

Living with less and stepping away from excessive consumerism changes you. It allows you to become the real you and follow your heart's desires, which you may have neglected for a while. Time with family and friends will never seem so precious. But most of all, you can slow down and appreciate the wonders of your life, dreaming of all those unknown adventures that are yet to come.

PART 1

Getting *prepared*

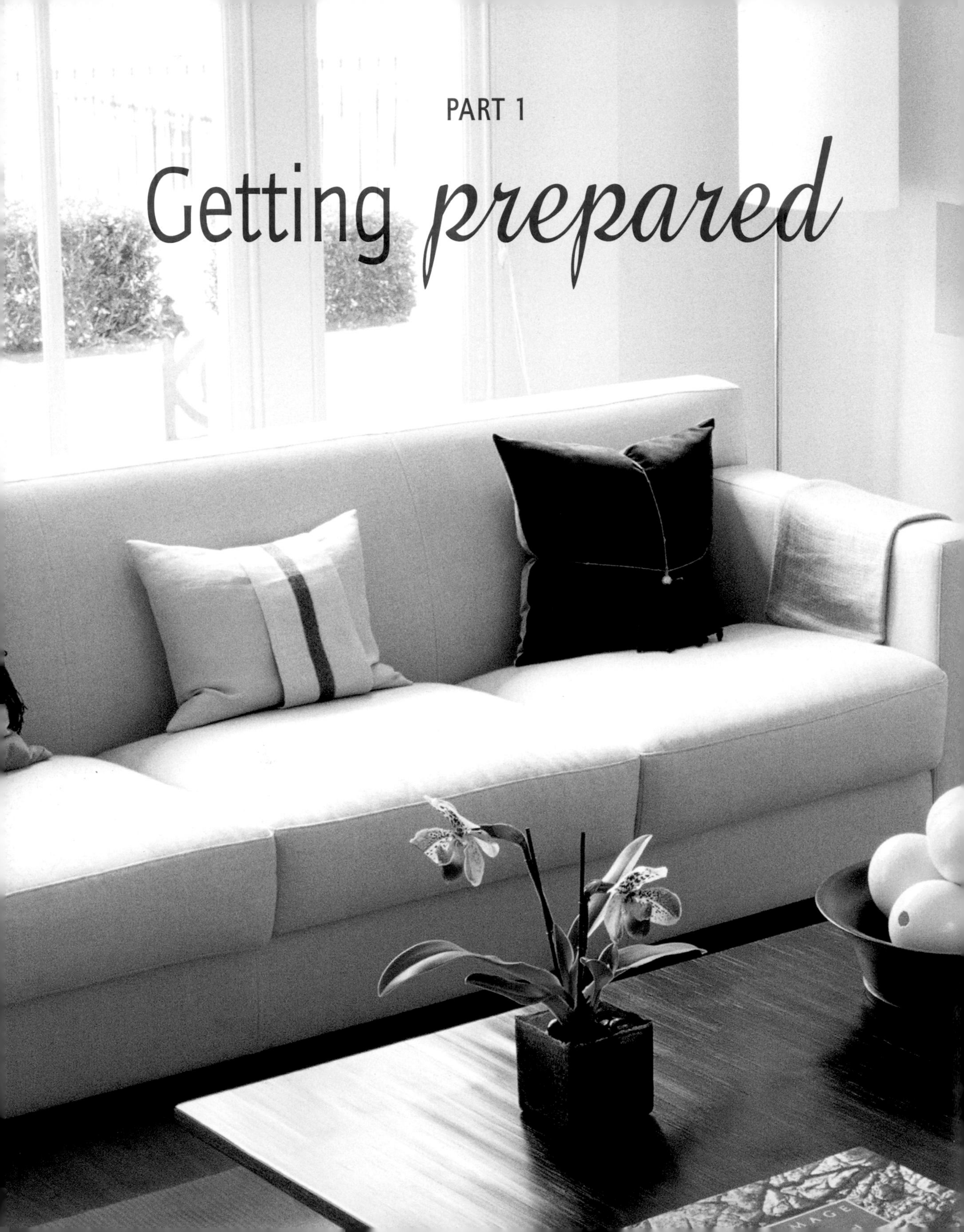

Taking on the challenge of living with 100 items is a big ask for most of us, since consumerism plays such a major part in western society today. In fact, many people have a buying addiction, whether it is for clothes or something else, but anyone tempted to buy in the pursuit of happiness soon finds out that the joy is merely fleeting. Here we explore how consumerism has become such a major part of our lives—so much so that some people hoard possessions as a comfort blanket to replace emotional contentment. Getting into the frame of mind to let go of possessions that you have kept for a long time is hard to do, but once you start releasing them, your life changes phenomenally. Your home is no longer cluttered, the atmosphere feels vibrant, and you feel inspired to try out new activities and spend more quality, happy times with friends and family.

WHAT TYPE *of consumer* are you?

We all love material possessions, and consumerism is not actually the problem. The trouble is over-consumerism. If a love of owning things turns into an obsession, it can fuel a constant need to buy the latest gadget, advertised household product, or "must-have" dress. People often think that by buying these things they will find the happiness they seek, but generally the opposite happens. A buying "fix" can provide a quick "high" but the emotional downturn kicks in pretty soon.

How about you? Do you look around your home and see piles of rarely used bits and pieces? This can feel overwhelming and create a stifling atmosphere, making the quest for a simpler, more minimalist life extremely appealing.

Buying on credit

One of the innovations that transformed our buying habits was the introduction of the credit card. American Express launched their card in 1958, closely followed by the BankAmericard (now Visa). By the early 1960s Mastercard had arrived, and it was promoted as timesaving rather than as a form of credit. Both American Express and Mastercard became instant successes. Barclaycard, the first UK credit card, was launched in 1966.

It wasn't long before a credit card was an accepted way to pay for goods and services, and everyone had at least one. This is fine if you pay off your card or cards each month, but if you don't, with high interest rates, it is very easy to build up debt.

Have you ever worked out what you are spending on your personal shopping each month? It can be scary how easy it is to buy that new coat, phone, or pair of shoes. The worry is can you really afford them? But more to the point, do you really need them?

CREDIT CARD DEBT

How many credit cards do you have and use regularly? In the US the average is four, while in the UK it's two. Since it is so easy to buy with a credit card, it is not surprising that the average individual debt is $15,799 in the US, and £2,324 in the UK. Debt is accepted as normal. In fact, research done by the charity Shelter in August 2011 in the UK found that 6 percent of the 2,200 people contacted had used credit cards to pay their monthly mortgage, compared with 4 percent in November 2009. This suggests that more than two million people are fighting just to keep a roof over their heads.

Does advertising fuel consumerism?

Advertising sells new products but is it brainwashing us all? There is no doubt that we see a huge number of advertisements each year. In fact, a 2004 survey for the Federal Trade Commission in the US on childhood obesity discovered that the average child aged 2 to 11 watches more than 25,000 TV adverts a year, while the average adult watches 52,500. This means that children spend a week every year, and adults spend two weeks, just watching television advertisements.

So how does this affect us? Inevitably, watching so many product advertisements encourages an image of "the good life" and visions of what can make us happy. The downside is that these same advertisements can

bring a sense of dissatisfaction with what we have, and make us want more. When parents cannot afford the things their children see advertised, this can lead to feelings of inadequacy.

But isn't shopping supposed to be fun? Because of this, many people are often willing to go into debt so that they can buy the latest camera, or toy for their child. Even in tough times, when budgets are tight and consumers are cutting back, they will still spend a large amount on gifts for special occasions, such as birthdays and Christmas, just increasing their debt.

Has over-consumerism had its day?

People have always "dropped out" of society but there seems to be a growing trend in both Britain and the United States toward a simpler lifestyle, maybe in reaction to over-consumerism. A slower pace of life is possible away from busy towns, and a degree of self-sufficiency has its attractions. More and more people are growing their own produce and keeping hens. Often environmentally aware, they are also investigating ways to save energy and water with different methods of consumption. Other people, fed up with working long hours and seeing little of their families, leave their urban lifestyles behind and move to rural areas or go abroad, just to embrace a more relaxed and fulfilling way of living.

BUYING POWER

When credit cards were launched, consumers could suddenly buy goods and services without paying for them straightaway, which was much easier than under the old installment plan or hire-purchase system. Although this fueled debt, it created bigger markets for consumer goods and stimulated economic growth. The credit card companies charged interest on any debt not paid off each month. Certain consumer products soon became the norm for every household. Most British households owned a vacuum cleaner by the late 1950s, a washing machine by the 1960s, a car by the 1970s, and a cell phone by the 1990s.

By the early 2000s, everyone was having a love affair with buying and owning electronic goods, and in the US in 2007, 78 percent of the population owned a computer. By 2009, 70 percent of Britons owned one, too, while today the figure for both countries is nearer 90 percent. In 2007, cars, which were once a luxury, were owned by 77 percent of Britons, and 27 percent owned two. By 2009 in the US, only 8.8 percent of people didn't own a car—33.7 percent actually owned one, 37.6 percent owned two, and 19.9 percent owned three. By 2011, more than 90 percent of both Britons and Americans owned a cell phone and a DVD player.

Does living a simpler life appeal to you?

Are you fed up with the consumer-led society and having a cluttered home? If so, you may be dreaming of attaining a simpler lifestyle with fewer possessions. The aim of this book is to guide you on the path toward the happiness and fulfillment that is eluding you. You can leave behind excessive consumerism, but what are the benefits for you if you do decide to follow this route?

* **Less time spent caring for possessions.** The more goods you have in your home, the more time you spend mending, cleaning, and maintaining them. The constant cleaning of plastic, metal, or glass items can leave you emotionally and physically drained, especially if you don't need them, or even enjoy having them.

* **Less envy.** Today's media constantly show us the rich and famous at play, making us envious of their lavish lifestyles, which are well beyond our more limited incomes. By giving up excessive consumerism, you can reject wanting to live a more upmarket lifestyle.

* **Less environmental impact.** Many goods are packaged in plastic, which takes years to degrade. By reducing your buying, you are reducing the amount of packaging you are responsible for, and also the number of discarded articles that will need recycling.

* **Less need to keep up with modern trends.** By stopping yourself from constantly buying things that are not needed, you will reduce your desire to conform to the latest style, whether it be in fashion, decoration, or design.

* **More kindness.** If you turn your back on excessive consumerism, you will have more free time and energy, and more available money. You may decide to help others less privileged than yourself. Giving time or money to charities, or supporting good causes in the community, is far more satisfying than buying something new.

* **More contentment.** A simpler lifestyle allows you time to follow your dreams. You may take up that hobby that you have never previously found time for, passionately pursue a new sport, or just spend more time with your family and friends.

Making the decision to escape excessive consumerism and live with a limited number of possessions is not an easy one, or more people would do it. In this book I am holding your hand and helping you to face the challenge. The rewards are truly amazing. You will find an inner spiritual contentment that you just did not think was possible.

HOARDING *too many* possessions

Before you start your 100-item challenge and set off on the road to your minimalist lifestyle, even before you think about changing excessive shopping habits, you need to look at why you have acquired so many things in the first place.

In my profession as a feng shui and decluttering consultant, I have come across many homes so full of possessions that the family could hardly move around them—and it doesn't stop there. I am often shown a garage or shed that is equally full, mainly of junk that has been stored and forgotten about. When I question my clients about why they have accumulated so many things, the answer is usually vague, along the lines of "it just sort of happened", or "I don't like to waste things." After some more gentle probing, I often discover that at least one family member can't stop buying, or one is a complete hoarder.

Hoarders will hold on to things they do not really want or need. They are just obsessed with the need to buy and accumulate. Sometimes these people are information addicts who feel compelled to save newspapers, magazines, or brochures, so that when they have time, they can read all the useful information they believe to be contained in them. And they do not just hoard new items. When a close relative dies, for example, rather than keeping the odd personal memento, they keep the majority of their relative's things, making their own home a mausoleum to someone else's past.

DID YOU KNOW?

Hoarding can be an illness and there are around 6–15 million compulsive hoarders in the US, and around 1.2 million in the UK.

HOW HOARDING POSSESSIONS AFFECTS YOUR HOME

As a feng shui consultant one of the main things I do is improve the energy flow in people's homes; you might prefer to think of it as the atmosphere of the home. According to this ancient Chinese practice, an invisible life force—electromagnetic meridians of energy called chi—flows through all things. It is important that this life force flows positively through your home to create a good atmosphere, but if your home is full of clutter or is overloaded with possessions, the flow is inhibited, and this creates a very lethargic and stale atmosphere.

Another tenet of feng shui is that we all have an inner/outer reality. So if your home is full of junk and has stale energy, it will have an effect on you both emotionally and spiritually, making you feel down and lacking direction and focus in your life. When you finally let go of unwanted belongings that have been stored in your home for years, it is really liberating and can be like a breath of fresh air or a major spring-clean. This, in turn, will have a major effect on you, giving you new inspiration and a positive direction for your life.

Why do people hoard?

One of the major reasons is the feeling of security that hoarding brings. Some people become emotionally attached to the things around them. Looking at objects or other accessories that they have acquired over the years makes them feel happy and safe. Some even keep mementoes from unhappy events, refusing to remember the pain involved, or hang on to a gift that they dislike for fear of upsetting the person who gave it to them if they passed it on. Giving away or throwing out items they no longer need but to which they have an emotional attachment can be painful, tantamount to rejecting a friend's generosity.

Different types of hoarders

When friends choose gifts, they do so with a loving intention, and these feelings can become bound up in the energy of the objects, which is why it can be so hard to let go of them. Sometimes true hoarders feel that part of their identity is attached to their possessions, and that by giving them away they are losing part of themselves.

Depression or grief can also fuel buying sprees, and when this comes on top of a compulsion to own the latest gadget, despite having many more at home, belongings can start piling up to an overwhelming extent, making it more difficult to shift them.

Creative people often save things to further their art and can easily become hoarders. Often they accumulate so many art supplies that they get in the way of normal life and the art projects never get done.

* Clothes (often unworn with labels left on)
* Newspapers and magazines
* Containers
* Junk mail
* Books
* Craft items

Are *you* a hoarder?

This questionnaire will help you work out, ahead of your challenge, if you are hoarding too many possessions or unwanted items in your home. Score 2 points for a "Yes," 1 for a "Sometimes," and zero for a "No."

	Yes	Sometimes	No
1 Can you park your car in your garage, or is it too full of stuff?			
2 Are your bookshelves filled with books that you never read?			
3 Do you have piles of unread magazines and newspapers everywhere?			
4 Do you store unused or broken items under your bed?			
5 Are piles of junk mail left by your front door?			
6 Is your closet bulging with clothes that you don't wear?			
7 Is your purse, bag, or workbag full of old pens, receipts, candy wrappers, and other worthless trivia?			
8 Can you hardly get in your attic because you have so much stuff stored up there?			
9 Have you kept all your old school certificates or sports awards?			
10 Is your sock or pantyhose drawer so full you can hardly get it open?			
11 Do you have lots of framed photographs or art prints that have never been displayed stacked in a closet?			

	Yes	Sometimes	No
12 Do you still keep shoes or boots even if you don't like them any more, they are badly worn, or have broken heels?			
13 Are you storing sports or fitness equipment that has never been used?			
14 Are you keeping photographs (prints or digital versions) of people who are no longer friends?			
15 Are unfinished craft projects scattered around your home?			
16 Is your home office full of paperwork that you have never got around to filing?			
17 Do you have old cell phones or broken electronic equipment stored in your home?			
18 Is your computer full of undeleted emails from months ago?			
19 Do you dislike some of the accessories or pictures in your home but never quite get around to disposing of them?			
20 Do you have any presents from friends or family, stored in the attic or a cabinet, that have never seen the light of day?			
TOTAL			

THE RESULTS

30–40
Your hoarding tendencies are getting out of control. Start to look at ways of curbing your spending habits. You can now also pinpoint some of the key areas you will need to tackle first when you start the overall challenge of reducing all the possessions in your home. Become more ruthless in getting rid of things and ask yourself: Do I need, want, or use this?

20–30
Although hoarding is not a major problem for you, it could start to get out of control, so set a date to start offloading your superfluous possessions.

10–20
Hoarding is not a big issue for you yet. But do start looking at what you are willing to give away.

Below 10
You are not by habit a hoarder, so you should have no problem in releasing some possessions.

HOW to *become* more minimalist

This can be daunting at first, as you will peel away emotional layers, removing items you have hung on to for years, but you will find it spiritually rewarding, and you will reinvent yourself.

When you are going through the process of reducing all your belongings, and working on your 100-items list, focus on keeping the special things that remind you of happy times, and ones that you truly like or love, and use regularly—really think if you need that waffle pan or the jelly mold you use once a year! The problem with hoarding too many old things is that they will strongly link you to your past, and will stop new things or people coming into your life. Stripping back your possessions can affect you profoundly (don't underestimate it), and can make you realize what is truly important in your life.

You need to keep items around you that foster and represent your current self, not the person you were years ago—bear this in mind when you are making your choices. All your possessions have an "energy" and those that are neglected or not used give off a stagnancy that can depress you. But the positive energy that comes from wanted or cherished objects will inspire you, help with your growth, and support your current dreams or goals.

ARE *you buying* or *keeping possessions* to fill an emotional need?

This is something it's helpful to know before you start your letting go challenge. Score 2 points for a "Yes," 1 for a "Sometimes," and zero for a "No."

	Yes	Sometimes	No
1 Do you constantly buy new clothes to boost your self-confidence and promote your self-image?			
2 When you go through lonely periods or feel a bit unloved, do you find comfort in buying something?			
3 Do you buy a new item for that initial buzz, and later feel a bit empty?			
4 Is your attic full of mementoes of your grown-up children, such as toys, baby clothes and dolls, because you love to evoke happy memories of the past?			
5 Does being surrounded by accessories that have been in your home for years make you feel secure?			
6 Have you kept old love letters from previous partners, because when you read them again it makes you feel wanted?			
7 Do you feel that letting go of possessions, even magazines, is like losing a part of yourself?			
8 Do you keep cuddly animals on your bed and derive emotional comfort from hugging them at night?			

	Yes	Sometimes	No
9 Do you have clothes that you almost consider to be your friends and so can't bear to throw them out, even if they don't fit?			
10 Do you relish acquiring knowledge so much that you keep newspapers for months, because there is always something left in them to read?			
11 Are you addicted to auction sites, such as E-bay, because you love the excitement of buying, and of winning a bid?			
12 Have you got boxes of old birthday and Christmas cards that you look at occasionally to make you feel loved?			
13 Are your food cupboards bulging with cans and other items, because you worry you may not have enough to eat?			
14 Is your bathroom cabinet overstocked with rarely used medical supplies just in case one of the family gets sick?			
15 Are you reluctant to throw out old correspondence or bills, because you can feel part of your past slipping away?			
TOTAL			

THE RESULTS

20–30
You are investing far too much emotion in your buying habits and the possessions you already have. Before you start attempting to pare down your belongings and adapting your shopping habits, try to discover what has caused you to invest so much emotion in material things, and work on releasing these deeply felt ties.

15–20
You have some emotional connection to regular buying and to the items in your home, but it is not overwhelming you. However, don't go on buying trips when you feel emotionally vulnerable, and start preparing yourself mentally for the loss of possessions.

10–15
Having an emotional need for possessions is not a major issue for you but start developing a dispassionate attitude toward everything you own before your liberating task begins.

Under 10
You rarely buy emotionally and can distance yourself mentally from your belongings, so stay in this mindset when you begin to clear out.

LETTING *go*

You need to be in the right mindset to let go of a lot of your possessions, and getting there can be tough, especially if you have had these things for a long time. If your home is really cluttered, try to think why you have surrounded yourself with so many things. Has it made you feel more protected? Many people hang on to possessions they no longer need or want because they are symbolically wrapping themselves up in "cotton wool" so that they do not move on or progress in life. They may be doing this subconsciously, and once the possessions start to go, and these layers of "cotton wool" are removed, they can initially feel bereft and more exposed. But once they accept that the belongings have gone for good, a wonderful feeling of liberation can creep in. They no longer have to force themselves into cluttered rooms or spend hours searching for something that is hidden under piles of other stuff. If you have been feeling like this, just focus on all the new things you will be able to do when you have a clearer, more streamlined home.

Getting going

Taking on the 100-item challenge, and letting other household possessions go, is a big step and it has to be taken when you are in the right frame of mind. So mentally prepare yourself for letting go of goods that you have kept for years. Don't ever start this type of project when you are feeling emotionally down or have had an upset or an argument, because you will find it hard to let go of anything. Shortly before starting your challenge, choose a quiet weekend to look through old photo albums, pick up and hold accessories, and browse through some of the books on your shelves. Maybe spend some time trying on your old clothes and have fun remembering the old you, when you were younger, and the occasions when you wore the outfits. Allowing yourself time to reminisce about your belongings will make it easier to release some of them.

DID YOU KNOW? ··

There are around 50,000 self-storage units in the US. People move items out of their homes and into storage just to get organized, and the goods are left there on average for 38 weeks a year. The UK is further behind with 1,200 self-storage units.

Appraising your home

Now comes the harder part—going around your home and looking at everything in it with a dispassionate eye. Try to see it as a visitor would. Is it cozy but very cluttered? Do your books, CDs, and DVDs dominate your living room because you own so many of them? Do the countless accessories on the windowsill mean that you can hardly see the cherished pictures of your family and friends? Has your love of magazines resulted in piles of them scattered all around the living room and entry hall? Is your kitchen a welcoming place or are the counters so full of appliances and products that it just looks too busy. This is the "heart" of the home, where people love to gather and chat, and it should be warm and inviting.

Move into the bedrooms and note any boxes you have stored on top of the wardrobes. Are your clothes bulging out of the closets or drawers? Look under the beds—you may be surprised what forgotten junk has been stored under them. Are the toys in your kids' bedrooms out of control and scattered all around the room? Think when you last gave any away to thrift (charity) stores or hospitals. Is your bathroom a soothing, relaxing place, or does it irritate you with the number of beauty products it contains? And are these strewn all around the bath or shower? Is your home study a pleasant place to enter or is it so full of paperwork, stationery, and office equipment that you feel overwhelmed? What about the attic? Can you get into it easily or is it an assault course, full of items that have just been dumped there and not used for years?

As you tour your home, really look at all your bits and pieces and ask yourself: Do I really like or love them? Do I need them? You may be surprised at your reaction. Some item you once adored just may not appeal to you any more. Remember that we all change and develop over time, so if you are surrounded with possessions that are, say, five to ten years old, you can find a mismatch of energies. These items are holding you in a past that you need to leave behind. Surrounding yourself only with things that suit you and your family's current lifestyle will make you feel positive about yourself. It will give a boost to your energy and increase your self-esteem.

You may feel a bit depressed once you have assessed your home and realize how many possessions you have accumulated, but remember that it is in your power to change it all and create the new life for yourself that you want.

RELEASING OLD OR UNWANTED POSSESSIONS

Ask yourself the following questions and if you answer "Yes" to most of them, you definitely have items in your home that you need to release.

* Are there any items you have not used in the last year?
* Do you have several broken articles that have not been repaired?
* Have you got any inherited furniture that you dislike?
* Do you dislike any possessions?
* Do you have things in your home that you don't remember buying?

* Is your attic full of unwanted presents?
* Is it difficult to get into your attic space because it is so full?
* Have your children got more toys than they ever play with?
* Do you have books on your shelves that have never been read?
* Have you got drawers full of old cell phones, watches, or other paraphernalia?

Case studies

CLIENT: *Sue*

PROBLEM: **OVERLOADED CLOSET**

I was called in because Sue needed some help to declutter her extensive wardrobe of clothes. She knew she had many items that she just didn't wear, but I was amazed to find several outfits that she had bought for weddings and had worn just that once. She constantly bought new clothes when she was feeling emotionally down but often never wore them and then forgot she had them. I found several purchases that still had the price tag attached to them. My worst discovery was that she had accumulated 20 black cardigans (how many do you need?). Five of them were in their original packaging and had never been worn!

It took us two full days to work through Sue's clothes, releasing the ones that no longer suited her to thrift (charity) stores and putting some aside to sell in a secondhand designer shop. We then organized her wardrobe into categories so that she could easily find things. Sue promised not to buy any more clothes when she was upset and to make an effort to wear all of the ones she had kept.

CLIENT: *Deborah*

PROBLEM: CLUTTERED BEDROOM

Deborah was married with two children. Before she had her kids she had run a clutter-clearing business and was quite minimalist in her outlook, but her standards had slipped due to time pressures and a husband who liked living in disorganized chaos. I could hardly get into the bedroom because of the number of black trash can liners and plastic bags full of junk. How they ever slept in there I do not know. As we slowly went through the contents of each bag, we came across several new bottles of shampoo, conditioner, and shower gel—Deborah already had many replacements in the bathroom. Besides unwanted paperwork and junk for throwing out, we also found new vests, shirts, and socks for the children, which she had bought for the new school year but then lost in this crowded room. The ultimate find, under a pile of stuff, was a brand new Blackberry phone. It had got buried and her husband had just ordered another one without even thinking about it.

It took us all day to clear this one room. By the end, after many discussions about how she had got into this situation, Deborah had learned her lesson and resolved to work on reforming her husband's hoarding tendencies and never to let the clutter take over again. She also realized how privileged she was financially, and resolved to donate the new clothes we had found to a children's charity. The mass of bathroom and beauty products went to a sale at her children's school.

PART 2

The 100-item *challenge*

Can you imagine living with just 100 personal possessions? This is the ultimate challenge I am giving you to live a simpler and more minimalist lifestyle, where you don't feel obliged to rush out and buy the latest gadget or the most advertised piece of clothing. Making your list of personal possessions will highlight your buying weaknesses, and reducing it to 100 will force you to rationalize what is important to you. Setting separate goals for releasing your belongings is the ideal way to work through the challenge, so that you do not become too overwhelmed by the process. You will also feel good, knowing that either you will benefit financially from selling your possessions, or that you are helping others by donating them to worthy causes.

WHY *take on* the 100-item challenge?

Part of my role as a feng shui consultant is to help people declutter their homes, so I am used to the ethos of letting go of things you no longer need or want, and not overloading with possessions. However, when I decided to write this book and took on the challenge of trying to prune my own personal possessions down to 100, I must admit I was a bit worried. I live in Brighton, on England's south coast, and the proximity of the stores to my home means I can easily go shopping for clothes, and since I moved here, my collection of clothes has grown considerably. This is the area I was concerned about—

I love my clothes but am I really wearing all of them? And do they all reflect my current image? I do clear out quite regularly but I have fallen prey, like many people, to all the special offers on T-shirts and other items. My journey, including all my ups and downs, to get down to 100 personal possessions is related in my blog, which starts in this section of the book.

WHAT WILL I GAIN FROM DOING THE 100-ITEM CHALLENGE?

1 You will help to declutter your home.
2 You will have the goal of sticking to 100 personal possessions, even if you buy new things.
3 It will help you live a simpler, less stressful life.
4 It will make you focus on what possessions you feel are essential, what you love, and what you don't need.
5 You can have some fun testing your minimalist capabilities.
6 You will no longer be defined by your possessions.
7 You will be less obsessed with consumerism and will feel an improvement in your spiritual and emotional wellbeing.
8 Buying new items for the sake of it will become a thing of the past.
9 Your home will seem so much larger with more space in which to move around.
10 With fewer items in your home, the atmosphere will completely change and feel brighter and more uplifting.

Taking on the 100-item challenge is a positive step that will start you on the way to a simpler lifestyle with less stress and more time to contemplate your dreams and goals for the future. Having a picture of the life in front of you in your head, owning fewer possessions, will give you that impetus to get started.

Going around your home and really looking at everything you have will make you realize where your buying weaknesses lie. You may be a shopaholic for clothes, and love buying shoes, bags and purses, or jewelry. Maybe your obsession is your hobby and you love buying extras for your camera since photography is so important to you. It may prove hard at first but once you start shedding some of these possessions, you will start to feel lighter and happier as you lose the responsibility for looking after them. You will also notice an improvement in the atmosphere of your home, because having too many possessions creates a stagnancy, a dull atmosphere, that makes you feel sluggish and lacking in motivation. Removing a lot of them will bring about a positive shift in energy.

Are you worried about the challenge?

You may now be starting to get cold feet and feel a bit scared about the mammoth decluttering challenge you have ahead of you. "Do I really need to do it?" you may be asking yourself. It is a big undertaking but remember that you will find so much satisfaction in doing it, and you will start to appreciate other more important things in life. You may have felt for some time that you are on the consumer treadmill, constantly being encouraged to buy merchandise that you don't really need. Won't it feel good to come off that treadmill and relish other things in life? Too many of us have got into the habit of buying things in pursuit of contentment and happiness only to find emotional emptiness once the initial thrill has gone. And you don't need to buy the latest phone, TV, computer, or MP3 player—living with an older model of any of these for a while will free you up to spend money and time on the activities you truly enjoy.

Don't start to panic once you have started the challenge if you hear a voice inside your head saying, "What if I need this in the future?" This is your subconscious trying to trip you up. Just release the old item graciously. If you do need something similar in the future, buying a new version will keep much more positive energy around you.

Emotional benefits of the challenge

You will become much more aware of what is important to you. Removing a lot of possessions from your life is similar to going off trekking or traveling for several months at a time. By cutting down, you will focus on what clothes you love and feel are essential, as well as on other items you use regularly and feel you can't do without. It will also make you realize that your love of life doesn't come from having a lot of possessions but from the activities you do and the time you spend with your family and friends. If you love painting or drawing, you may discover how important your art materials are to you; or it may be your walking gear if you go on walking weekends with your local rambling group. You will find far more happiness in having a day out with your family, playing a sport, or catching up with girlfriends than going on a mammoth shopping trip.

You may well fall in love with your home all over again as you liberate it from clutter. Clearing out will give you more space, and it will have an effect on you too, clearing and energizing your mind. As you let go of possessions that you may have held onto for many years, you may feel inspired to start hosting dinner parties again, having a games evening, or perhaps be the venue for the next book club meeting.

As you progress through the challenge, you will find yourself developing a much more disciplined attitude to buying, and may even start to find that browsing around the stores is less enjoyable. The other gain from doing the challenge is that consumer items will have less appeal when you experience the joy of all your other activities. Remember, too, that this is a challenge for a set period of time and you may decide not to continue with it at the end. However, your buying attitude will have changed forever and you will find yourself looking much more carefully at every product that you are thinking about owning.

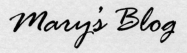

Mary's Blog

I can't believe that I am about to start my 100-item challenge. Clothes are going to be the hardest group to pare down, because I seem to have acquired so many more since I left London four years ago to live by the sea. It's only a ten-minute walk down to the shops in the trendy Lanes area of Brighton. Why do there have to be so many boutiques that just seem to call me in, knowing that I just love new boots, shoes, and bags? It's going to be a real test for me to be ruthless and let go of the ones I'm not using. I don't mind letting go of belongings, because decluttering is a regular part of my work, but it's so easy to clear out and then let stuff accumulate again. I will just have to keep saying to myself the mantra I say over and over to clients: Do I need it or want it? Once I start, I find letting go is quite easy, but I still hesitate over the odd cocktail or evening dress at the back of the closet. I don't wear them often now, but there might just be that special occasion... I will try them on and if I still look great in them, I will keep one or two.

   Hobbies are not really my thing but I was a good tennis player in my day and I am keen to keep my tennis racket for the odd game, even though I don't play much now. I love working out, and at my age it is essential to keep middle-age spread at bay, so I have quite a collection of workout gear that needs to be refined—do I really need that many T-shirts? I am feeling quite excited now but also a bit apprehensive about what's ahead. I know I will learn a lot from putting myself through this challenge.

Where did the 100-item challenge start?

The concept of living with 100 personal possessions was the idea of online entrepreneur Dave Bruno, who looked around his San Diego home one day in 2007 and decided that all his family's belongings were weighing him down. So began his quest, outlined in his blog at guynameddave.com, to reduce all his personal possessions to 100 items in a year. Although he reached his goal within that schedule, to date his slow and steady purge of items is still continuing.

The idea of living with fewer things is not new. Mahatma Gandhi (1869–1948), the non-violent leader of the Indian nationalist movement, adopted a very simple lifestyle, dressing in the clothes of an Indian villager. His own brief list of personal belongings included sandals, a plate, a bowl, his spectacles, and a pocket watch. More recently, in Britain, *Guardian* columnist Leo Hickman decided to work with the idea that a person needs just ten belongings (excluding essential clothing and household goods). His list included a Swiss army knife and a treasured painting by one of his children.

When I conceived the idea for this book, I wanted to bring in the idea of a 100-item challenge in a workbook style, so I could provide some guidance on decluttering, since this is one of my areas of expertise. Clearing out all unnecessary household goods is essential for changing a life of over-consumerism, but focusing on reducing your own belongings is a much harder test and a more personal experience. Letting go of your own possessions is never easy but once you start cutting that tie with them it can be liberating. When you release these surplus items, everything that you keep will have special meaning and purpose.

Don't give up!

You are going to hit some rough patches during the challenge. So if you are finding it tough letting go of your belongings, give yourself a day or two off and come back mentally revitalized and emotionally refreshed.

MAKING *your* 100-item list

I have been inspired to take on the 100-item challenge through my work as a decluttering consultant. Having seen many clients over the years who have filled their homes with too many possessions, I was curious to test myself and see how minimalist I could be with my personal belongings. By "items," or personal possessions, I mean all the items that you own and use, for example, your MP3 player, your computer, and your clothes. All household goods that are used by your family and friends, such as furniture, electrical items in shared areas, and china, are excluded from the challenge. However, some of these still need to be cleared out, and advice on decluttering every room is covered in Part 3 of the book.

Taking on the challenge is a strict discipline but it is also fun and will highlight how much money you can waste buying what are basically unwanted or frivolous goods. The challenge is also about acquiring a more spacious, clutter-free home, and having more spare time and money to pursue the activities you love.

How to organize your list

Remember, this is a challenge that is good for the soul, so you can set your own rules, provided that you keep to them for your specified time. You may decide to try it for a year or 18 months and then review it. It is also your choice how to count items. It is sensible to group some. You may decide that your collection of purses (handbags) is so huge that it's best to group them as one, but nevertheless, always aim to reduce the number that you have. It is also a good idea to group all underwear, and socks and pantyhose as one item, or you will never achieve your 100 items! I have decided to group my shoes as one item but will cut back on my collection. Achieving your 100 items will make you feel very self-disciplined.

When making your list, leave some room for gifts that may come your way. You can still buy clothes or new items, as long as they don't put your list over 100, and you can replace anything that's worn-out or broken. You can also allow yourself one indulgence that is excluded from the challenge. Mine is going to be my jewelry collection. I just love bright crystal pieces to match my outfits.

So whether you are single, one of a couple, or part of a family, before you get going set some ground rules.

What is excluded

* All general or shared household items. This means furniture, such as sofas, chairs, and beds, and electrical items, such as televisions, DVD players, fridge/freezers, stoves, microwaves, and kettles
* All china and glasses
* All basic food items
* Tool kits and home repair (DIY) items
* Books
* DVDs and CDs
* Household cleaning materials
* Soft furnishings and bedlinen
* Stationery and home-office furniture and supplies
* Cars
* Shampoos, conditioners, and other shared bathroom products

What is included

* Clothes: general items, nightwear, shoes, sandals, boots, gloves, coats, jackets, scarves, belts, ties, hats, and wraps
* Jewelry
* Cosmetics, including nail scissors, nail varnishes, and tweezers
* Toothbrushes, razors, aftershaves, perfumes, and moisturizers
* Personal hair dryer, hair straighteners, and curlers
* Personal computer, laptop, and printer
* Cell phone, camera, electronic items, including tablets, e-readers, game boys, PlayStations, and Xboxes
* Watches, clocks, penknives, sunglasses, and spectacles
* MP3 players, headphones, and docking stations
* Hobby items, such as personal musical instruments, photography equipment, train sets, sketch pads and paints, and craft and knitting kits
* Bicycle or motorbike and helmet
* Suitcases, purses, backpacks, bags, workbags, and wallets
* Notepad, journals, pens, and pencils
* Sports gear, such as tennis rackets, golf clubs, surfboards, football gear, running equipment, and skateboards

These lists are just a guide so if you have something personal that is not here and you feel should be included, add it in.

THE 100-ITEM CHALLENGE

WHAT *possessions* can't you live without?

Fill in this questionnaire to find out what are your essential items.
Score 2 points for a "Yes," 1 for a "Sometimes," and zero for a "No."

	Yes	Sometimes	No		Yes	Sometimes	No
1 Does your MP3 player have to go everywhere with you?				12 Is it upsetting to find you have no time to change your purse (bag) to match your outfit?			
2 Are you completely lost without your laptop?				13 Is your camera always in your bag, just in case you spot something fascinating to photograph?			
3 Do you have special boots that you always choose to wear?				14 Do your friends recognize you from a distance, because you always wear the same jacket when you are out?			
4 If you lost your cherished leather jacket, would you be mortified?				15 In the summer, are you lost if you leave your designer sunglasses behind?			
5 Do you freak out if you realize that you have left your e-reader at home?				16 Is your gym bag always packed and ready for your next workout session?			
6 If your beloved black trousers are in the wash, are you at a loss for what to wear?				17 Do you regularly rotate three or four shirts or T-shirts to wear?			
7 Do you start to panic if you can't find your smart phone?				18 Are you at a loss if you can't find your notebook and pen to make notes to yourself?			
8 Are you constantly checking all your meetings and arrangements in your diary?				19 Do you keep your golf clubs, tennis racket, or squash racket by the door, ready for the next game?			
9 Does your makeup bag have to go everywhere with you so that you can easily touch up your lip gloss or mascara?				20 Do you feel almost undressed if you don't wear your preferred hat when you go out?			
10 Do you take your backpack with you at all times, and feel lost without it?				TOTAL			
11 Do you wear the same piece or pieces of jewelry every day?							

THE RESULTS

30-40
You have a lot of possessions that are an essential part of your life. Since all of these count toward your list of 100 items, you may need to toughen up so that you are ready to release other less important belongings. Focus on what you really want and need in your life.

20-30
Although your list of loved belongings is not enormous, the 100-item challenge will still be tough, so start to get into the mindset of letting go of all your unnecessary possessions.

10-20
Attachment to personal possessions is not a huge problem for you, but start reviewing which ones you really want to keep.

Below 10
You do not seem to have too much attachment to your belongings, and should find the challenge quite easy to undertake.

TAKING *an inventory* of your personal possessions

Before you can start the challenge, you need to take an inventory of all the things you own that you alone use, and start noting down your feelings about releasing them. Remember that general household goods are excluded from this list (see page 39.) Allow some time, because it can take a while to log everything. You may be horrified at how much you have accumulated or pleasantly surprised that it is not as much as you thought. Maybe start on a quiet weekend.

Before you make your list, decide what possessions you are going to write down individually, and what you are going to group together as one item, to make your task easier. For example, are you going to list your shoes and boots pair by pair or as one or two groups? Are

you going to put your purses (handbags) down separately or as a group? Men may decide to put ties and belts down as one or two group items. It's your decision. As women will generally have more possessions, I think it's sensible to make more group items if it means that you will keep to the challenge.

Write your list on a large lined pad and have a selection of colored pens, including black, so you can color-code your decisions about what to keep and what to move on. When you have finished, pin the pad somewhere you will see it every day, such as on the fridge door.

Where to begin?

I suggest you start in your bedroom, if that is where you keep your clothes, because they will make up around 70 percent of your challenge items. List them all, including footwear, using a black pen—this is all your summer and winter clothes, and your fat and thin clothes, if you have them! If any are stored in boxes on top of the wardrobe or under the bed, add them in as well. Don't forget to include any clothes that you wear infrequently, such as ski wear or cocktail or evening dresses, which may be stored away in the attic. All your coats, jackets, scarves, and hats, which may be hanging downstairs or by the front door, should be included, too.

If you are struggling to make decisions about what to keep and what to lose, it may be an idea to invite a girlfriend for the afternoon to help you decide. Try things on to get her opinion. A friend who is not emotionally involved with your clothes will be able to say more honestly what flatters you and what doesn't suit you or, possibly, fit you any more. Remember, this is your inventory so you can have several "don't knows" if you need more time to let go of some old favorites.

While in this room, add in any electrical items, such as hair dryers, hair straighteners, shavers, or alarm clocks that are personal to you. Don't forget to make it clear what are your essentials that you can't do without. If female, add your cosmetics, perfumes, purses (handbags), bags, and jewelry to the list.

All your other belongings

Move on from your bedroom and note down all your personal electronic items, such as laptops, mobile printers (exclude big home-office equipment, like a fax machine or photocopier), cell phones, MP3 players, e-readers, and tablets. If you have several old models, note these down and mark them as "can go"—you can probably sell them or pass them on (see pages 44–45.)

Look at any hobby items you may have. Do you have lots of craft equipment and tools, say for making rugs of jewelry? They all need to be recorded. If you are a sports lover, all your equipment must be listed—tennis rackets and balls, hockey sticks, weight-training kit, skateboards, and any other gear must be added.

Finally, add the small miscellaneous possessions—your wallet, penknife, sunglasses, notepad or journal and pen, watches, even your toothbrush. If you have a bicycle or motorbike, add it in.

If you are feeling a bit shell-shocked by the length of your list, don't forget you can still exclude one indulgence item or group from your challenge. Also, remember the aim of the challenge is to get down to 100 items, but if you get stuck at 150, store the ones you just can't relinquish in the attic or a closet until the end of the challenge. If you have missed them, you may well get them out again, but if not, move them on.

Check through your list and make sure you haven't left anything out before filling in the current personal possessions list on pages 52–55, followed by your proposed list of 100 items on pages 56–57. You are now well on the way to achieving your new minimalist lifestyle.

pages 52–55 ... pages 56–57

DID YOU KNOW?

* One woman in ten in the US is willing to spend $150 on a purse (handbag). The average number of purses (handbags) owned by an American woman is 21.
* Women in the UK spend on average £4,000 over a lifetime on purses (handbags). The average number owned by a British woman is 17. Around two-thirds of the women surveyed said they would like to buy more!

Tip

To focus your mind, think of the precious possessions you would save if escaping from a fire.

While you are taking your inventory of all your clothes, gadgets, and other belongings, write next to each item in red if it is a "must have," in blue for a "don't know," and in green for "can go." You may find that a lot of the "can gos" appear next to clothes. Other items, such as your laptop, are probably essential to you. When you start the Goals section (see pages 62–81), review the list and make your final decisions to get down to your 100 items.

Clothes

Winter

- ✔ Black jeans
- ✘ Black jeans
- ✔ Blue jeans
- ✔ Red jeans
- ✘ Long black skirt
- ✘ Black and red skirt
- ? Black and red skirt
- ? Orange and black dress
- ✔ Black and white dress
- ✔ Pink jersey dress
- ✔ Violet jersey dress
- ✘ Red sweater
- ✘ White sweater
- ✘ Pink sweater
- ? Orange long-sleeved T-shirt

Summer

- ✔ Red dress
- ✔ Red and white dress
- ✘ Floral dress
- ? Brown and pink dress
- ? Green patterned skirt
- ✔ Mauve and pink skirt
- ✔ White T-shirt
- ✘ Red T-shirt
- ✔ Pink T-shirt

Gadgets & miscellaneous

- ✔ Laptop
- ✔ Printer
- ✔ iPhone
- ✔ iPod and headphones
- ✔ Camera
- ✔ Hair dryer
- ✔ Hair straighteners
- ✔ Moisturizer
- ✔ Deodorant
- ? Black watch
- ✘ Silver watch
- ✘ Black purse
- ✘ Black purse
- ✘ Beige evening purse
- ✘ Pink evening purse
- ✔ Sunglasses
- ? Sunglasses
- ✔ Bicycle
- ✔ Bicycle helmet
- ✔ Bicycle gloves
- ? Wallet
- ✔ Wallet
- ✘ Wallet
- ✔ Toothbrush
- ✘ Medium suitcase
- ✔ Small suitcase

Mary's personal items

FIRST INVENTORY This is my list of personal possessions just before starting my 100-item challenge (excluding all household items.)

Gadgets & miscellaneous

1 Laptop
2 Old computer
3 Printer
4 iPhone
5 iPod and headphones
6 iPod docking station
7 Hair dryer
8 Hair straighteners
9 CD player for meditation discs
10 Purse/wallet
11 Purse/wallet
12 Purse/wallet
13 Filofax
14 Sunglasses
15 Sunglasses
16 Spectacles
17 Black watch
18 Silver watch
19 Black watch
20 Jewelry (this will be my indulgence)
21 Camera
22 Tennis racket and balls
23 Bicycle helmet
24 Bicycle gloves
25 Bicycle

26 Art materials
27 Hand mirror
28 Hair brush
29 Hair brush
30 Hair brush
31 Moisturizer
32 Deodorant
33 Bag of cosmetics
34 Perfumes x 3
35 Razor
36 Washbag
37 Toothbrush
38 Penknife
39 Pen
40 Black handbag (purse)
41 Black handbag (purse)

42 Black handbag (purse)
43 Black handbag (purse)
44 Black handbag (purse)
45 Tan handbag (purse)
46 Maroon handbag (purse)
47 Brown handbag (purse)
48 Brown handbag (purse)
49 White handbag (purse)
50 Beige handbag (purse)
51 Black evening handbag (purse)

52 Black evening handbag (purse)
53 Black evening handbag (purse)
54 Black evening handbag (purse)
55 Brown evening handbag (purse)
56 Beige evening handbag (purse)
57 Pink evening handbag (purse)
58 Basket
59 Patterned basket
60 Patterned basket
61 Orange basket
62 Brown basket
63 Pink work bag
64 Black work bag
65 Brown briefcase
66 Red backpack
67 Clock
68 Large suitcase
69 Medium suitcase
70 Medium suitcase
71 Small suitcase
72 Small suitcase
73 Soft bag

Clothes

Winter

74 Black jeans
75 Black jeans
76 Blue jeans
77 Blue jeans
78 Red jeans
79 Stone jeans
80 Black trousers
81 Black trousers
82 Black leggings
83 Black leggings
84 Blue skirt
85 Multicolored skirt
86 Pink and black skirt
87 Dark blue skirt
88 Brown patterned skirt
89 Long black skirt
90 Black and red skirt
91 Black and red skirt
92 Orange/black dress
93 Black/white dress
94 Muticolored dress
95 Red/black evening dress
96 Brown and blue dress
97 Gray and black evening dress

98 Pink jersey dress
99 Violet jersey dress
100 Green sweater
101 Red sweater
102 Red sweater
103 White sweater
104 Pink sweater
105 Beige sweater
106 Red long-sleeved top
107 White long-sleeved top
108 Brown striped long-sleeved top
109 Brown patterned long-sleeved top
110 Orange long-sleeved T-shirt
111 Orange long-sleeved T-shirt
112 Burnt orange long-sleeved T-shirt
113 Pink long-sleeved T-shirt
114 Pink long-sleeved T-shirt
115 Red long-sleeved T-shirt

116 Red long-sleeved T-shirt
117 Red long-sleeved T-shirt
118 Mauve long-sleeved T-shirt
119 Mauve long-sleeved T-shirt
120 Blue long-sleeved T-shirt
121 White long-sleeved T-shirt
122 White long-sleeved T-shirt
123 White long-sleeved T-shirt
124 White long-sleeved T-shirt
125 Pink/brown evening top
126 Green evening top
127 Maroon evening top
128 Dark mauve evening top
129 Red evening top
130 Gray fleece
131 Blue fleece

132 Red fleece
133 Pink light fleece
134 Panties (about 20)
135 Bras (about 10)
136 Brown belt
137 Brown belt
138 Brown belt
139 Brown belt
140 Brown belt
141 Black belt
142 Black belt
143 Brown/silver belt
144 Brown boots
145 Brown boots
146 Beige boots
147 Beige boots
148 Black boots
149 Black boots
150 Black boots
151 Black boots
152 Green/brown boots
153 Sneakers (trainers)
154 Black shoes
155 Black shoes
156 Brown winter coat
157 Black winter jacket
158 Black winter jacket

Mary's personal items *continued*

Clothes

Summer

159 Black and white dress
160 Black patterned dress
161 Red and white dress
162 Red dress
163 Red dress
164 Red dress
165 Pink dress
166 Blue and pink dress
167 Floral dress
168 Brown and pink dress
169 Bikinis/ swimsuits x 5
170 Red sandals
171 Red sandals
172 Brown slip-ons
173 Brown flip-flops
174 Brown flip-flops
175 Brown flip-flops
176 White sandals
177 Black sandals
178 Black sandals
179 Black sandals
180 Black sandals
181 Brown sandals
182 Brown sandals
183 Brown sandals

184 Swimming shoes
185 Black/white dotted skirt
186 Gray patterned skirt
187 Blue and red skirt
188 Pink and mauve skirt
189 Pink skirt
190 Green and red skirt
191 Green patterned skirt
192 Green patterned skirt
193 Mauve and pink skirt
194 White T-shirt
195 White T-shirt
196 White T-shirt
197 Gray T-shirt
198 Red T-shirt
199 Red T-shirt
200 Red T-shirt
201 Red T-shirt
202 Blue T-shirt
203 Blue T-shirt
204 Blue T-shirt
205 Mauve T-shirt
206 Peach T-shirt
207 Pink T-shirt
208 Green T-shirt
209 Green T-shirt
210 Long gray cardigan
211 Long mauve cardigan

212 Blue cardigan
213 Pink cardigan
214 Pink patterned cardigan
215 Green cardigan
216 White cardigan
217 Beige cardigan
218 Brown cardigan
219 Cream cardigan
220 Red cardigan
221 White cropped pants (trousers)
222 White cropped pants (trousers)
223 Blue cropped pants (trousers)
224 Green vest T-shirt
225 Pink vest T-shirt
226 Red vest T-shirt
227 Red vest T-shirt
228 Peach vest T-shirt
229 White vest T-shirt
230 White vest T-shirt
231 White vest T-shirt
232 Light pink vest T-shirt
233 Mauve vest T-shirt
234 Mauve vest T-shirt

235 Light green vest T-shirt
236 Orange vest T-shirt
237 Orange vest T-shirt
238 Yellow vest T-shirt
239 Pink vest T-shirt
240 White strappy T-shirt
241 White strappy T-shirt
242 Pink strappy T-shirt
243 Pink strappy T-shirt
244 Pink strappy T-shirt
245 Pink patterned strappy T-shirt
246 Red strappy T-shirt
247 Mauve strappy T-shirt
248 Yellow strappy T-shirt
249 Blue strappy T-shirt
250 Cream strappy T-shirt
251 Orange strappy T-shirt
252 Beige strappy T-shirt
253 Beige strappy T-shirt
254 Blue strappy T-shirt
255 Dark green shorts
256 Beige shorts
257 Beige shorts
258 Beige shorts

259 Yellow shorts
260 Pink shorts
261 Blue shorts
262 Red shorts
263 White cover-up
264 Black gym shorts
265 Black gym shorts
266 Gray gym shorts
267 Black gym leggings
268 Black gym leggings
269 Red gym shirt
270 Maroon gym shirt
271 Pink gym shirt
272 White gym shirt
273 White gym shirt
274 White gym shirt
275 Green gym shirt
276 Black jacket
277 Cream jacket
278 Black leather jacket
279 Short black leather
    jacket
280 Short brown jacket

General

281 Rain jacket
282 Rain jacket
283 Scarves (about 12)
284 Wraps (about 6)
285 Pantyhose and socks
    (about 12 in all)
286 Blue patterned
    nightdress
287 Blue nightdress
288 Blue nightdress
289 Blue nightdress

290 White nightdress
291 Red and cream
    nightdress
292 Pink pjs
293 Pink pjs
294 Pink striped pjs
295 Pink slippers
296 Pink bathrobe
297 Pink and white
    bathrobe
298 Black hat

299 Brown hat
300 Beige hat
301 Leopard-skin band
302 Black gloves
303 Black leather gloves
304 Brown gloves
305 Brown leather gloves

Total 305 items

Mary's 100-item list

I am giving myself a year to get down to this level. I think that shedding some unworn clothes and unused items is going to be quite easy, but getting down to just 100 is going to be a real challenge. I have grouped several things together to help me with my list. I haven't managed to leave any space for presents, so will just have to ask for replacements.

Gadgets & miscellaneous

1   Laptop
2   Printer
3   iPhone
4   iPod and headphones
5   iPod docking system
6   Hair dryer
7   Hair straighteners
8   CD player for meditation discs
9   Purse/wallets x 2/Filofax
10 Sunglasses x 2
11 Spectacles
12 Watches x 3
13 Camera
14 Tennis racket and balls
15 Bicycle helmet and gloves
16 Bicycle
17 Art materials
18 Hand mirror
19 Hair brushes x 3
20 Moisturizer
21 Deodorant
22 Perfumes x 3
23 Razor
24 Bag of cosmetics
25 Washbag
26 Toothbrush
27 Penknife
28 Handbags (purses) x 10
29 Evening bags (purses) x 4
30 Baskets x 3
31 Workbags x 3
32 Suitcases x 3

Clothes

Winter

33 Black jeans
34 Blue jeans
35 Black pants (trousers)
36 Black pants (trousers)
37 Black leggings
38 Blue skirt
39 Multicolored skirt
40 Pink and black skirt
41 Brown patterned skirt
42 Dark blue skirt
43 Dresses x 7
44 Green sweater
45 Red sweater
46 Beige sweater
47 Red long-sleeved top
48 Burnt orange long-sleeved
   T-shirt
49 Pink long-sleeved T-shirt
50 Red long-sleeved T-shirt
51 Mauve long-sleeved T-shirt
52 Blue long-sleeved T-shirt
53 White long-sleeved T-shirt
54 Pink/brown evening top
55 Dark mauve evening top
56 Blue fleece
57 Red fleece
58 Panties (about 13) and
   bras (about 10)
59 Belts x 6
60 Boots and sneakers x 7
61 Brown winter coat
62 Black winter jacket
63 Black winter jacket

Summer

64 Dresses x 9
65 Bikinis/swimsuits x 5
66 Sandals x 13
67 Swimming shoes
68 Black/white dotted skirt
69 Gray patterned skirt
70 Blue and red skirt
71 Pink and mauve skirt
72 Mauve and pink skirt
73 T-shirts x 13
74 Cardigans x 10
75 White cropped pants (trousers)
76 Vest T-shirts x 12
77 Strappy T-shirts x 11
78 Dark green shorts
79 Beige shorts
80 Black gym shorts
81 Gray gym shorts
82 Black gym leggings
83 Red gym shirt
84 Maroon gym shirt
85 Black short jacket
86 Cream jacket
87 Black leather jacket
88 Short black leather jacket

General

89 Rain jacket
90 Scarves and wraps x 11
91 Pantyhose and socks x 16
92 Blue patterned nightdress
93 Blue nightdress
94 Blue nightdress
95 Pink pjs
96 White/pink slippers
97 Pink bathrobe
98 Pink and white bathrobe
99 Hats x 4
100 Gloves x 4

Total 100 items

Your current list of personal items

FIRST INVENTORY Fill in your inventory list here, and total up what you have at the bottom, as I did (see page 49.) Don't forget to exclude all household goods and to group underwear, and pantyhose and socks. If you have too many possessions to fit on these two spreads, continue on another piece of paper but write the totals at the bottom on page 55.

Gadgets & miscellaneous

Winter clothes

Summer clothes

Your current list *continued*

Gadgets & miscellaneous

Winter clothes

Summer clothes

_____   _____
_____   _____
_____   _____
_____   _____
_____   _____
_____   _____
_____   _____
_____   _____
_____   _____
_____   _____
_____   _____
_____   _____
_____   _____
_____   _____
_____   _____
_____   _____
_____   _____
_____   _____
_____   _____
_____   _____

Gadgets & miscellaneous

Total

Winter clothes

Total

Summer clothes

Total

Total items

Your 100-item list

Remember you can allow yourself up to a year, or longer, to achieve this number. The main reason for compiling this list is to get into the mindset to let go of things. Group items together if you are finding it just too hard. It is your challenge and you can make your own rules.

Gadgets & miscellaneous

Winter clothes

Summer clothes

Total

HOW DO *lists* vary between women and men

I think it is generally much harder for women than it is for men to reduce personal possessions down to 100. We just seem to have so much more stuff. Our bedrooms are full of purses (handbags), cosmetics, hair dryers, numerous pairs of shoes, jewelry, belts plus all our other bits and pieces. Most of us have a lot of clothes because we just love dressing up and looking good. Have you noticed, for example, when you go through security at an airport with just hand luggage, all the women's plastic bags of liquids are bulging with cleansers, moisturizers, cosmetics, deodorant, shampoo, conditioner, and perfume, while the men's bags seem to have about four items: shampoo/conditioner, toothpaste, deodorant, aftershave, and possibly a moisturizer if he is really looking after himself! I thought I had been so clever on my last trip with hand luggage to see my sister in Portugal, when I put some perfume in a small container. But when I arrived, I discovered that the air pressure had "glued" on the top of the container, and the perfume had evaporated!

Women, while not so interested in gadgets, are often inseparable from their smart phone, MP3 player, and e-reader. Hair dryers and straighteners are also high on their "must-have" list. Many women love creative pastimes, enjoying art or craft classes, and also take part in various sports. Keep-fit sessions are very popular. Aerobic classes, dance classes, or yoga or pilates tend to be favored rather than muscle-building training in the gym. Women often spend money on having the latest coordinating workout gear, as do men.

Women attempting the challenge of living with just 100 items need to focus on the possessions that make their hearts sing.

So how do men differ?

Men generally seem to be more frugal with their possessions (except when it comes to gadgets). They usually have fewer clothes than women, although they can be obsessed with collecting some items, such as T-shirts from rock concerts. As a rule, they dress more for functionality, and are not so drawn by the need to purchase the latest fashions as are women. How often have you heard that a man is happy wearing the same pair of jeans or jacket for weeks on end? Would you ever see a woman doing that? Some men are even quite happy to let their partners buy their clothes for them. However, they can have a tendency to hang on to old suits that no longer fit and keep a collection of ties that are hardly worn. And although men may well take care of their appearance, having regular haircuts and shaving every day, they do not seem to want, or need, numerous skin-enhancing products in the same way as women.

Technology lovers

One of the main differences between the sexes, though, is that men have a tendency to collect things: football or baseball cards, train sets, old records, military memorabilia, classic books, and comics can be popular. They are lovers of electronic gadgets and enjoy keeping up with the latest models, often pre-ordering the latest iPhone, iPad, e-reader, PlayStation or Xbox. Technology seems to fascinate them, whereas women just do not have the same interest or awareness. Playing sports and keeping fit is also high on their list of interests. Running, hiking, climbing, working out in the gym, cycling, and playing football are just some of the favorites. And this is where they go against their normal lack of interest in buying clothes. Men often love buying the latest and most expensive sports gear and sneakers.

Men attempting the challenge of living with just 100 items will have to decide what gadgets, clothes, and hobby materials they just can't live without.

Mary's Blog

My bedroom looks like a bombsite! Practically everything I own is scattered around as I look through everything. I have just read that the average British woman has 22 items of clothing that she never wears but refuses to throw out because of the guilt of wasting money! Thankfully, that is not my problem, but I have just discovered two black Tula bags in the top of my closet that I haven't used in over a year, so they are going to the secondhand store that has just opened at the end of my road—maybe I can earn some cash from them? Apparently, too many of us buy clothes for our slimmer, sexier persona, and they just end up sitting at the back of the closet. I am not guilty of that but I do love those offers on T-shirts...

Out, too, go my beige boots that seem to have worn down more on one foot than the other, making them so uncomfortable to wear now. My black biker boots can go as well—they just don't seem to be me any more. Oh good, a charity bag for breast cancer has just come through the door. I can fill it up with my reject scarves plus a waterproof jacket and some other bits. Still a long way to go, but it does feel good donating things I no longer need to a good cause.

DID YOU KNOW?

The gadgets that most men and women say they can't do without are phones, such as the iPhone and Blackberry smart phones, MP3 music players, laptops, cameras, watches, and e-readers, such as the Kindle. Women also put hair gadgets, such as hair dryers, straighteners, and curlers, high on their list. For men, tablets, such as the iPad and game stations, are near the top of the list.

COMPARING a *Man's* and a *Woman's* 100-item list

There seem to be several quite obvious differences between the proposed lists compiled by an average man and woman. Men generally seem to love gadgets. Hobby and sports items for the outdoors are more important to them than they are to women, and they have a much more functional list of clothes. Women, on the other hand, aren't normally so obsessed with gadgets, besides cell phones, have a much more extensive range of clothes, bags, and shoes, but are less interested in hobby or sports goods. It is intriguing to compare the different lists, so have a look again at my final list (see pages 50–51) and contrast it with my friend Paul's list (opposite).

Mary's Blog

I'm just coming back on the train from seeing a client in London and I'm surrounded by men either using their iPads or typing furiously on their laptops. Do they ever switch off? I'm exhausted and listening to my iPod, but I suppose that's just another gadget... I am still working hard on reducing my clothes. Out went my long black skirt that never seems to get worn nowadays—the parties I go to are much more casual. As I put the dress I wore to my nephew's wedding into a bag for the secondhand store, I fondly remembered the occasion six years ago. Simon and Emma got married in a wonderful evening ceremony, by candlelight, in the garden of a glorious old building in Valencia, Spain, where they were living at the time. I paid a lot for the dress but have rarely worn it.

   Okay, now I am letting go of a pair of black shoes, some black sandals, and some brown flip-flops.

Gadgets & miscellaneous

1   Laptop
2   Digital camera
3   Blackberry phone
4   iPad
5   iPod touch and headphones
6   Headset, no microphone
7   Wallet
8   Watch
9   Sunglasses
10 Wedding ring
11 Electric razor
12 Toothbrush
13 Guitar
14 Penknife
15 Deodorant
16 Aftershaves x 3
17 Tweezers
18 Notebook and pen
19 Backpack
20 Suitcase
21 Tent
22 Sleeping bag
23 Surfboard
24 Wetsuit
25 Giant road bicycle

Clothes

Winter

26 Blue jeans
27 Blue jeans
28 Blue jeans
29 Brown suit
30 Black pants (trousers)
31 Tan pants (trousers)
32 Black chinos
33 Tan chinos
34 Blue long-sleeved shirt
35 White long-sleeved shirt
36 Black long-sleeved shirt
37 Brown long-sleeved shirt
38 Gray long-sleeved shirt
39 Blue button-down shirt
40 Gray button-down shirt
41 Belts x 3
42 White sweater
43 Gray sweater
44 White Argyle sweater
45 Gray Argyle sweater
46 Gray tank top
47 Red tank top
48 Old gray football jersey
49 Blue sweatshirt
50 Gray hooded fleece
51 Navy blue hooded fleece
52 Gray down jacket
53 Black coat
54 Brown sports jacket
55 Brown shoes
56 Black shoes
57 Casual brown shoes
58 Running shoes
59 Hiking boots

Summer

60 Beige linen jacket
61 Gray short-sleeved
    button-down shirt
62 Blue short-sleeved
    button-down shirt
63 Pink short-sleeved
    button-down shirt
64 Beige short-sleeved
    button-down shirt
65 Gray T-shirt
66 Black T-shirt
67 Red T-shirt
68 Green T-shirt
69 Blue T-shirt
70 White T-shirt
71 White T-shirt
72 Gray vest T-shirt
73 Black vest T-shirt
74 White shorts
75 Brown shorts
76 Beige shorts
77 Black shorts
78 Dark blue shorts
79 Blue and white
    swimsuits x 2
80 Brown sandals
81 Blue flip-flops

General

82 White gym shirt
83 White gym shirt
84 Gray gym shirt
85 Black running shirt
86 Black running shorts
87 Black running shorts
88 Gray sweatpants
89 Gray sweatpants
90 Undershirts x 5
91 Socks x 8
92 Underwear x 10
93 Striped pjs x 3
94 Striped toweling bathrobe
95 Rain jacket
96 Scarves x 2
97 Gray hat
98 Black baseball cap
99 Black gloves
100 Brown gloves

Total   100

GOAL *setting*

Now you have planned your 100-item list, how are you going to achieve it? Setting goals within a time scale is the best way. If you are not good at letting things go, you may find this quite difficult to do but, I promise you, you will feel better at the end of it. Refining your possessions down to those that you really love and want can focus you both mentally and emotionally. And what are all those things that you never use doing? Basically, they are just gathering dust and using up space in your home. Too often people hang on to things they do not use or want through inertia or lethargy—they have just got used to those things being there. By moving them on, you will create an atmosphere that is much more positive and vibrant, which everyone in your family will notice and appreciate. Also, exciting new things can come into your life after a clear-out, when the energy in your home is boosted.

Making your plan

To keep on track, make sure the goals and time limits you set yourself are achievable. A year is a good target to set. If you feel you can do it in less time, that's fine, but if you are really overloaded with stuff, you may feel 18 months is more realistic. I have set myself a year to reach my target of 100 items. I think I will get there more quickly than that but may get stuck on losing the last 50 items, which I still love and want to keep. Work out your goals chart (see the sample chart opposite,) print it out with the timings involved, and display it in a prominent place where you will see it every day. As you reach each goal, cross through it with a colored pen and feel that sense of achievement. If you are feeling a bit daunted, think of it as a fun game where you are testing yourself to see how few things you can live with.

If you are working to a year's schedule, make sure you plan how many months to allow for reducing your collection of clothes, for example. In my sample plan, I suggest that Goal 1 should be working on your clothes; Goal 2 can be your shoes, boots, bags, wallets, and suitcases; Goal 3 your jewelry, cosmetics, perfumes, aftershaves, and miscellaneous possessions;

and Goal 4 your electronic items. Goal 5 can be your sports goods, and Goal 6 your hobby materials. If you have other things that do not fit into these categories, just add them to your chart. As your clothes will make up about 70 percent of your final list of 100, it is a good idea to allow more time to clear out your closet. Adopt the mantra "love it, use it, or lose it" for everything you own to help you make your decisions.

Sample goal-setting chart

You will find it helpful to display your chart on your fridge door, on the closet in your bedroom, or in any other prominent position where you can't ignore it. Decide your start month and how many months you are giving yourself to work on the first goal, then fill in the next goal, and so on. If you find you are going to need more time to complete each goal, just change the dates on your chart. In this example I have allowed 4½ months to pare down clothes and 1½ months each for the other more minor goals.

		Start date	Completion date
1st goal:	All clothes	end July	mid-December
2nd goal:	Shoes, boots, wallets, purses, bags, suitcases	mid-December	end January
3rd goal:	Jewelry, cosmetics, miscellaneous possessions	end January	mid-March
4th goal:	Electronic items	mid-March	end April
5th goal:	Sports equipment	end April	mid-June
6th goal:	Hobby materials	mid-June	end July

GOAL 1: clbthes

TIME TO COMPLETE: 4½ months

This is your first goal and the biggest part of your 100-item challenge because it deals with all your clothes, which will make up a major part of your list. I have allocated a fair bit of time to achieving this goal, but once you start removing clothes from where you store them, you may find you can complete the task more quickly. You may have decided to leave filling in your proposed list of 100 items (see pages 56–57) until you have worked through these clearing-out goals.

Getting rid of clothes you have had for a while can be quite a difficult process. They remind us of the happy times when we wore them. As you sort through them you may remember an event such as your sister's wedding or a party where you had a great time.

Clothes can often seem like friends because they are so much a part of us. They represent our personal style, and the image we are projecting to the world. However, letting go of clothes you no longer need or want can be liberating, and can stop you from being too tied to the past or to the person you were a few years ago. It is also worthwhile noting that most of us regularly wear just 20 percent of our clothes; the rest just hang in the closet, filling up space. If you weaken at any time, don't forget that the focus of this challenge is to make yourself question the role of consumerism in your life.

Letting go

To start the process of living with fewer clothes and having a "capsule" wardrobe of your favorite items, get together some heavy-duty trash bags. Label the first bag "Thrift (charity) store and friends" (you may need several of these). Label the second bag "Clothes to sell." If you have some really old clothes, you may want to add a third junk bag labeled "Clothes to throw out." Inviting friends to a clothes-exchange party can be a fun idea, so label another bag "Clothes to exchange."

Now look at the inventory you made earlier (see pages 52–55) and, following the checklist order below, start working through your clothes. Allocate a few hours at a time and stop when you feel you can't do any more. Start with the "can go" clothes on your inventory and put them in the appropriate black bags. Next, start work on your "don't know" list of clothes. You may have tried on some of these but still can't make a decision about letting them go. Give yourself a bit of time—it's not an easy process. You may have to come back to some of these on another day if you can't make up your mind. Finally, look at your "must have" list of clothes. You may find when you total up all of these that you still have too many for your 100 list and will have to refine them even more.

Once you have let go of your clothes and they are bagged up, make sure you move them on quickly, to the thrift (charity) or secondhand store, for example, or the temptation will be to start rooting through the bags again and putting some things back in the closet. Your subconscious will try to convince you that you can't possibly do without that particular dress or pair of pants!

Tip

Keep holding in your head the mantra

"love it, use it, or lose it"

as you sort through all your clothes.

Checklist

To keep you on track, it can help to go through your clothes in a set order, otherwise you may become overwhelmed by the task ahead. If you don't have any of the clothes in one of the sections listed, just skip to the next one. If you have something to add, just write it on a piece of paper. Go through both your winter and summer clothes at the same time.

Men

1 Suits
2 Shirts
3 Ties
4 Pants
5 Jeans
6 Long-sleeved T-shirts
7 Sweaters/sweater vests
8 Short-sleeved shirts
9 Short-sleeved T-shirts
10 Vest T-shirts
11 Shorts
12 Cropped pants
13 Cardigans
14 Fleeces
15 Socks
16 Underwear
17 Pjs
18 Bathrobes
19 Gym shorts/pants
20 Gym T-shirts
21 Swimsuits
22 Coats
23 Jackets
24 Rain jackets
25 Scarves
26 Hats
27 Gloves
28 Belts
29 Miscellaneous

Women

1 Skirts
2 Dresses
3 Shirts
4 Pants
5 Jeans
6 Long-sleeved T-shirts
7 Sweaters
8 Short-sleeved shirts
9 Short-sleeved T-shirts
10 Vest T-shirts
11 Strappy T-shirts
12 Shorts
13 Cropped pants
14 Cardigans/shrugs
15 Fleeces
16 Evening tops
17 Pantyhose/socks
18 Bras
19 Panties
20 Pjs
21 Nightdresses
22 Bathrobes
23 Gym shorts/leggings
24 Gym T-shirts
25 Bikinis and swimsuits
26 Coats
27 Jackets
28 Rain jackets
29 Scarves and wraps
30 Hats
31 Gloves
32 Belts
33 Miscellaneous

Too many clothes?

Now that you are looking at all your clothes and deciding what to keep and what to let go, it is interesting to look at the reasons why so many women, in particular, hang on to clothes they do not wear. Many women have a vast collection of clothes of all types and colors, so how is it that, according to statistics, most of us wear just 20 percent of all the clothes we own? Do we buy clothes for the sake of it and then forget about them? Is it laziness? Do we just wear the clothes that are nearest in the closet and forget about the rest? Do we buy too many clothes and forget what we have? Or is it that some don't fit or we just don't like them any more? Perhaps some people feel more secure with

more clothes to choose from, but whatever the reason or reasons may be, isn't it a waste of money to have so many clothes that are not worn? I know that when the weather is cold in the winter, I can easily just rotate between two pairs of jeans and two or three sweaters if I'm feeling lazy.

I decided to conduct an experiment among my friends by asking them to keep a winter clothes diary over a working week. I wanted to see if they wore a mixture of clothes and shoes or boots, or chose the same ones regularly, and if the reason for that was because it required less effort. Have a look at the results below.

MOVING CLOTHES ON

* Thrift (charity) stores. Many charities run stores and welcome donations of clothes in good condition. In the UK, charity bags, which can be filled with clothes, are often posted through your door (see page 87).
* Regular as well as designer secondhand stores. These will take good-quality clothes. You may be able to find a secondhand designer store for your designer label clothes (see page 84).
* Online auction sites, such as E-bay (see page 86).
* Exchange parties. Get together with friends and have a sociable evening looking through the clothes on offer. Anything left can go to a thrift store.

How are you doing?

Letting go of clothes you have had for a long time can be quite draining because we form such an attachment to them. Give yourself regular breaks, and praise yourself for what you have done at the end of each clearing-out session.

Emotional benefits of clearing out:
By keeping only the clothes that you like and look good wearing, you will boost your self-esteem and confidence. And giving clothes away to a worthy cause will make you feel good about yourself.

Sarah F.

Sarah is a clinical researcher.
This is her clothes list on a week off work.

Monday: Stripy blue/black top, blue baggy jeans, black knitted sweater, mid-leg buckled black boots.
Tuesday: Priscilla T-shirt, black knitted sweater, baggy blue jeans, black and white Converse sneakers.
Wednesday: Purple T-shirt over black long-sleeved top, gray denim skirt, black leggings, mid-leg buckled black boots.
Thursday: Purple T-shirt over gray long-sleeved top, gray denim skirt, black leggings, mid-leg buckled black boots.
Friday: Black lacy top, pleated brown skirt, thick black pantyhose, mid-leg buckled black boots.

Sarah wears a lot of black but has incorporated quite a few different clothes into her week's wardrobe. However, she has worn the same black boots on four days, and Sarah possesses ten different pairs of boots!

Mary's advice:

Sarah needs to wear her other boots or give them away or sell them. It would also be a good idea to wear some more colorful clothes because black can make you depressed.

Sue

Sue is a lawyer and regularly has to appear in court on behalf of clients.

Monday: Gray dress, black cardigan, black shoes.
Tuesday: Gray dress, black cardigan, black shoes.
Wednesday: Navy pin-striped suit, black shoes.
Thursday: Black suit, black top, black shoes.
Friday (day off): Blue jeans, gray sweater, black shoes.

Sue needs to look smart for her work but does seem to wear dark or muted colors, mainly gray and black, despite owning more colorful dresses and skirts. She also wore the same pair of black shoes on all five days.

Mary's advice:

Sue needs to wear more of a variety of clothes from her wardrobe; again more color is needed. I know she looks great in red! She also needs to vary the color of her shoes more.

Anna

Anna works in a London office as an accountant.

Monday: Blue dress, black knitted jacket, black ankle boots.
Tuesday: Printed skirt, black T-shirt, black ankle boots.
Wednesday: Black shift dress, black knitted jacket, black ankle boots.
Thursday: Black jeggings, black T-shirt (different one), black knitted jacket.
Friday: Blue jeans, green top, full-length black boots.

Anna wore several black pieces of clothing, and has chosen few colorful items for her weekly wardrobe. She also wore the same pair of ankle boots for four days in the week.

Mary's advice:

The same theme again. Anna needs to wear more of the boots and shoes in her wardrobe or move them on. Black is smart but wearing her colorful tops or skirts will boost her energy.

Sarah T.

Sarah works in marketing and generally works in an office during the week.

Monday: Brown polo neck sweater, brown pants, bright orange cardigan, brown suede boots.
Tuesday: Gray polo neck sweater, gray pants, red wrap-style cardigan, gray flat shoes in patent leather.
Wednesday: Brown polo neck sweater, brown pants, bright orange cardigan, brown suede boots.
Thursday: Black fleck pant suit, green sweater, black high boots.
Friday: Gray polo neck sweater, gray pants, lilac cardigan, gray flat shoes in patent leather.

Sarah repeats clothes in her week's selection. She also admits she chooses clothes that are easy to find on dark winter mornings.

Mary's advice:

Sarah could be more versatile with her choices, and wear more of her other tops and coordinates. Choosing her clothes the night before will solve finding things on dark mornings.

Lucy

Lucy works from home as a holistic healer.

Monday: Black jeans, animal-print top, long black cardigan, black boots.
Tuesday: Black leggings, green T-shirt, animal-print tie cardigan, black boots.
Wednesday: Black jeans, animal-print T-shirt, long black cardigan, black boots.
Thursday: Black jeans, stripy T-shirt, long black cardigan, black boots.
Friday: Black leggings, knitted animal-print dress, black boots.

Lucy regularly chooses black clothes as an easy option. There is also a big emphasis on animal prints, despite owning many other different styles. She also chose to wear the same pair of black boots all week.

Mary's advice:

Lucy needs to wear more of the other boots and shoes in her wardrobe for variety. Again some more colorful tops and cardigans would be a good idea.

A woman's wardrobe

Appraising your wardrobe before embarking on the 100-item challenge can take a while for a woman. You may find your closet is full of clothes that you do not wear, some hidden, still with their labels on, plus other items that are too tight and no longer fit.

The idea of the challenge is to pare down your wardrobe to only the clothes that you love and want, clothes you feel good in and wear regularly. Once you have sorted your clothes, you can color-code them as shirts, skirts, pants, and dresses, so that they can be easily picked out and matched together, particularly on those dark winter mornings. All the unwanted clothes can be passed on to friends or thrift (charity) stores, or sold through secondhand stores or online.

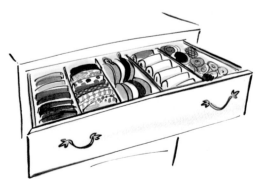

A man's wardrobe

A man also needs to take a good look at his wardrobe of clothes before starting the 100-item challenge. If you are not a tidy individual, there may be piles of clothes at the bottom of the closet to sort through. Sports shirts and old, holey sweaters may have been discarded and forgotten about. Some pairs of jeans and jogging pants may have seen better days and now need to go.

The challenge's purpose is to keep only the clothes that you wear often and love, the clothes that are stylish and which make you feel good about yourself. Be ruthless and throw out or pass on to thrift (charity) stores the clothes you dislike, or which no longer fit or are just worn out. Discard the gray underpants and the single socks that have lost their matching partner. Again, after your clearout, think about color coding your clothes in sections, keeeping all the pants, shirts, T-shirts, and jackets together, so that you can easily pull them out on those rushed mornings when you are trying to get to work early.

GOAL 2:
shoes, boots, bags, wallets, and suitcases

TIME TO COMPLETE: 1½ months

The second goal of your 100-item challenge is to deal with all your shoes, boots, purses (handbags), bags, wallets, and suitcases. I find this goal quite hard, because I love my collection of bags. I will have to be really tough with myself to let go of the ones I'm just not using any more. I also seem to have acquired a suitcase for every occasion—how many do you need? I will just have to be realistic and keep only the ones I use. Less time is needed to achieve this goal vbecause there are fewer possessions to deal with.

Shoes, boots, purses, and bags are an emotive area for most women. We love looking and feeling good,

and the right shoes and purse (handbag) can make an outfit special. But if you have bought freely for years, your closets are probably full of shoes, boots, and bags that you haven't worn or carried for a while. Do you remember that famous scene in *Sex and the City* when Carrie realizes she could have paid a deposit on a new apartment with the money she had spent on buying new designer shoes? You may feel you still love a lot of these possessions but if you are not using or wearing them, they are just cluttering up your bedroom. They may also relate to the "old" you, who possibly liked bolder styles than you do today. Throwing out battered

shoes, purses (handbags), and bags, and taking those that are in good condition to thrift (charity) or secondhand stores will make you feel good and create a workable collection that relates to your current style and energy. There is less emotion attached to wallets, suitcases, or workbags, but you still have to make your final selection.

Letting go

As with your clothes, use heavy-duty trash bags (see pages 64–65) and label them appropriately. Work swiftly through your inventory (see page 45), looking at your "can go" list, then your "don't knows," and finally your "must have" items. Use the checklist to keep you focused but change the heading to "Goal 2." You may also need a third bag labeled "Miscellaneous—to throw out."

Checklist

Go through all your shoes, boots, purses (handbags), bags, wallets, and suitcases in this order, and avoid flitting between closets and drawers.

1 Shoes (all formal and casual styles, high heels, and flats)
2 Boots
3 Sandals, flip-flops, swimming shoes
4 Sneakers, running shoes, walking and hiking boots
5 Purses (handbags)
6 Small evening bags
7 Wallets
8 Workbags
9 Backpacks
10 Suitcases or travel bags
11 Miscellaneous accessories, such as sunglasses and spectacles

How are you doing?

If you are stuck over certain possessions, go out for a brisk walk to clear your head.
Emotional benefits of clearing out:
Having less will make you fully appreciate the belongings you have kept.

MOVING BELONGINGS ON

✱ Thrift (charity) stores (see page 87).
✱ Secondhand stores and designer label secondhand stores (see page 84).
✱ Online auction sites, such as E-bay (see page 86).
✱ Car boot or garage sales (see page 86).

GOAL 3:
jewelery, cosmetics, and miscellaneous items

TIME TO COMPLETE: 1½ months

Your third goal is mainly female-orientated, involving sorting out jewelry, cosmetics, and other miscellaneous bits and pieces. I love my jewelry so have made it my indulgence, but I am still going to sort through every piece and make sure I still love and wear it, or I will pass it on. Having too many cosmetics is not really an issue for me. I use organic makeup and have quite a small amount. Again, this goal has a shorter completion time because there are fewer items you need to go through.

Most women love having jewelry to complement their outfits. A stunning necklace, bracelet, or ring makes you feel special. But today it is all too easy to buy cheap costume jewelry on a whim, and then rarely wear it. So if your jewelry box and hanging trees are overflowing, you may need some time to look through everything and decide what to keep. If you have some gold pieces that you never wear, selling them can be a good option since gold usually fetches a high price. You may come across items you have been given as presents that stimulate happy memories, or make you feel emotional, but hard as it is, try to put emotion aside. As with everything else, focus on what you love wearing, and which pieces make you feel good. Don't forget to include all your watches.

With cosmetics, the aim is to end up with just one makeup bag for all the eye shadows, eye pencils, liquid liners, blushers, brushes, mascaras, nail varnishes, creams, and lotions that you use regularly. Go through your makeup bag and get red of all those clogged-up old cosmetics, as well as any that are stored elsewhere. Don't forget to sort through your moisturizers and perfumes, or, if you are a man, aftershaves, as well.

Checklist

Keep focused by working through your jewelry and cosmetics in this order.

Jewelry
1 Necklaces/pendants
2 Bracelets/anklets
3 Earrings
4 Watches
5 Miscellaneous jewelry

Cosmetics
6 Eye shadows/creams
7 Blushers and brushes
8 Touch-up creams/ foundations/powders

9 Mascaras
10 Eye pencils/liners
11 Lipsticks/lipgloss
12 Moisturizers/serums
13 Nail varnishes
14 Miscellaneous items plus nail scissors, tweezers, and eyelash curlers
15 Fragrances

Refining your collection

With this goal I suggest using a couple of small boxes (something like a shoe box) for your jewelry. Label one "Thrift (charity) store and friends" and label the other "Jewelry to sell." Have a junk bag labeled "Cosmetics, lotions, and fragrances to throw out."

Work through your inventory (see page 45,) going through your "can go" list, "don't knows," and your "must have" items, although in this section you may have left it until now to make final choices.

How are you doing?

Letting go of possessions is draining, so pace yourself by doing a couple of hours at a time.
Emotional benefits of clearing out:
You will be amazed at how good you feel letting go of jewelry and cosmetics no longer needed.

LOVE IT, use it, or lose it

MOVING BELONGINGS ON

* Thrift (charity) stores (see page 87).
* Online auction sites, such as E-bay (see page 86).
* Jewelers (see page 85).
* Gold stores (see page 85).

GOAL 4:
electrical and electronic equipment

TIME TO COMPLETE: 1½ months

Your fourth goal may be a problem for men who love their electronic gadgets. I have not acquired too many of them but the challenge has spurred me on to sell my old cell phone and to give my old computer to a charity that will re-use it and clear your hard drive at the same time. Again, there is a shorter time to reach this goal because of fewer gadgets to review.

Electronic gadgets are the obsession of the 21st century. When a new version of a gadget, such as Apple's iPad, is announced, people often queue overnight to make sure they are among the first to own it. So what has fueled this demand for new gadgets? Is it material consumerism gone mad? Or is it just a fascination for new technology? There is no doubt that modern electronic appliances ease the running of our daily lives but there is also the slight worry that we can never switch off, because we are always contactable. If you are looking at the electrical and electronic items you own and wondering how to

reduce them for this challenge, try to think what you use or play with daily, and what is indispensable. Most women find it hard to be parted from their hair dryers, straighteners, or curling tongs, so these will probably be on their "must have" lists. Try to stay focused on how you are streamlining and simplifying your life when doing this challenge.

DID YOU KNOW?

The desire for new gadgets does not wane. According to a survey conducted at the end of 2011 by www.bing.com, the following items were the most wanted electronic items that year:

1 Xbox 360
2 Kindle Fire
3 Sony PlayStation
4 Apple's iPhone 5
5 Apple's iPad

6 Nintendo Wii
7 Apple's iPad 2
8 Nook digital reader
9 Windows Phone 7
10 Apple's MacBook Pro

MOVING BELONGINGS ON

✻ Thrift (charity) stores (see page 87).

✻ Online auction sites, such as E-bay (see page 86).

✻ Secondhand stores, such as Cash Converter
   (see page 86).

✻ Specialist websites buy old cell phones
   (see page 85).

Checklist

Use this list to go through all your current devices
and electrical appliances in order.

1	Computers/laptops	11	PlayStations
2	Printers	12	Portable CD/DVD
3	External hard drives		players
4	Cell phones	13	Electric razor
5	MP3 players and	14	Hair dryers
	headphones	15	Hair straighteners and
6	Docking stations and		curling tongs
	speakers	16	Miscellaneous gadgets
7	Separate headphones		including clocks
8	E-readers		
9	Tablets		
10	Xboxes		

Releasing gadgets

As this goal involves appliances, find some boxes
and label them "Thrift (charity) stores and friends"
(not all stores accept electrical and electronic
devices), "Gadgets to sell," and "Gadgets to
throw out."

Go through your inventory (see page 45),
starting with your "can go" list followed by
your "don't knows." You may struggle here,
feeling unsure whether to
release once-loved
appliances—give yourself
time to let them go.
When you are ready,
move on to your "must
have" devices.

GOAL 5:
sports and exercise equipment

TIME TO COMPLETE: 1 ½ months

Your fifth goal is to check your sports equipment. I don't play that many sports so sorting through these particular possessions is not too difficult for me. I still love tennis, and plan to keep my tennis racket and balls, even if I'm not playing much nowadays. My bicycle is a "must have"—one of the pleasures of living in Brighton is cycling by the sea during the summer months. Six weeks is the time allowed for this goal, which should be ample to rationalize all your sports paraphernalia.

For sports lovers, this is decision time. You may be keeping some equipment that you just don't use any more. Did you take up a sport, such as badminton, but gave it up after the initial enthusiasm wore off, and left the racket now languishing in your attic? Or maybe you tried canoeing or sailing but discovered that a life on the water wasn't for you? All this wasted equipment can be sold on auction websites, such as E-bay.

Alternatively, you can donate it to a youth club or sports club, who will appreciate the gift of hardly used equipment. By giving these things away, you will not only end up with your favorite items, creating good energy in your home, but you will also feel good about helping others.

Liberating sports equipment

Use some heavy-duty trash bags (see pages 64–65.) Label one "Youth club, sports club, or friends," and label another "Sports goods to sell." For any old unused equipment, label a third bag "Sports goods to throw out."

Tackle the sports section of your inventory (see page 45), starting with your "can go" list, and then move on to the "don't knows"—just release unused sports items. Lastly, sort out all your favorites in the "must have" selection.

How are you doing?

If you are slowing down because of remembering past sporting successes, ask a friend around, who will be less emotional, to help you de-junk.

Emotional benefits of clearing out:
You can let go of regrets for any sporting failures and look forward to future achievements in your best sports.

Checklist

Sort through your sports and exercise equipment as listed, to keep you on track with your clear-out.

1 Tennis rackets and balls
2 Badminton rackets and shuttlecocks
3 Squash rackets and balls
4 Golf clubs and golf balls
5 Skateboard
6 Surfboard
7 Running equipment
8 Weight-training belts and dumbbells
9 Hockey stick
10 Football and equipment
11 Swimming equipment
12 Bicycle
13 Cycling gear
14 Motorbike
15 Motorbike equipment
16 Aerobics/workout gear
17 Yoga mat and equipment
18 Pilates kit
19 Hiking or walking gear
20 Sailing kit
21 Camping equipment
22 Canoeing gear
23 Miscellaneous sports equipment, including penknives

MOVING BELONGINGS ON

* Thrift (charity) stores (see page 87.)
* Online auction sites, such as E-bay (see page 87.)
* Car boot/trunk or garage sales (see page 87.)
* Sports clubs or youth clubs (see page 84.)

GOAL 6:
hobby materials

TIME TO COMPLETE: 1½ months

The final goal of your 100-item challenge is to review your hobby materials. All those odd bits and pieces, such as your Filofax, notepad, or journal, are also included with this goal. I am not a great hobby person but I do really love drawing and painting, so these art materials are among my "must haves." Sketching outside is one of my enjoyments. I also love photography but never seem to find much time to take pictures.

Hobbies can be addictive—once you take up one, you just want to start more. But if you get bored quickly, it will mean that you have a lot of half-finished projects around. You may have tried a ceramics course, making jewelry, or maybe something like stained-glass work. Photography is an amazing hobby but you can acquire a lot of equipment that you may not get around to using. Perhaps you thought you were going to develop your own black-and-white prints and bought all the materials but then never had the time? All this kit is taking up space in your home. If you are an amateur musician, you probably have several instruments that you have bought over the years, but do you still play them all? When did you last play that guitar or keyboard? E-bay, other online auction sites,

Checklist

Work through all your hobby items in this order
to speed up the process.

1 Art materials
2 Craft kits
3 Gardening kit
4 Ceramic materials
5 Photography equipment
6 Stamp collections
7 Glass-making kits
8 Jewelry-making kits
9 Knitting paraphernalia
10 Sewing kits
11 Language disks
12 Guitar
13 Keyboard/piano
14 Trumpet
15 Saxophone
16 Flute/recorder
17 Train sets
18 Miscellaneous musical
   instruments
19 Journals, notepads, and
   pens
20 Diaries/Filofaxes
21 Miscellaneous hobby
   items

and secondhand stores are ideal places to sell on
unwanted expensive hobby items. Or you could donate
some cameras or musical instruments to amateur
clubs, which would really appreciate them. Helping
people can be incredibly rewarding, and can make
you appreciate how lucky you are and how much you
have in your life.

Relinquishing hobby materials

Again, use some heavy-duty trash bags (see pages
64–65,) label one "Amateur clubs or friends," and
another "Hobby equipment to sell." For any old craft
or hobby items, label a third bag "Hobby materials to
throw out."

Sort through your inventory (see page 45), moving
through your "can go" list, your "don't knows," and,
finally, check through your "must have" pieces.

How are you doing?

It can be difficult letting go of once-loved musical
instruments or photography equipment, so be
kind to yourself and don't do it all in one day—
let go gradually.

Emotional benefits of clearing out:
You may feel sad at letting go of these possessions
but think how happy you will feel using the hobby
equipment you truly want.

MOVING BELONGINGS ON

* Thrift (charity) stores (see page 86).
* Secondhand stores for musical instruments and
   photography equipment (see pages 84 and 85).
* Online auction sites, such as E-bay (see page 86).
* Car boot or garage sales (see page 86).

Case study

John
ARTIST

When John's marriage split up, the divorce was complicated and he found himself unable to buy a new property. At first he rented a room in London and later moved to Brighton on the south coast. John was used to living in a detached house with plenty of rooms, so he really had to think about what to take with him and what was important to him. He knew he couldn't take all of his clothes, so he sorted through them and managed to fill five black trash bags to take to a thrift (charity) store. John had recently taken up flying light aircraft but again this was one of the casualties of the divorce. However, he was not willing to let go of his other loves: painting and playing music. In the loft room that he rents, John has a set of acrylic paints and brushes, a set of oil paints and brushes, and some easels. He owns 12 didgeridoos, eight guitars, one tenor recorder, one cello, two banjos, one lute, one harmonica, one tin whistle, one synthesizer, and an electric piano.

Leaving behind his large house and dealing with the breakdown of his relationship was a huge wrench for John and he was then forced to prioritize what possessions to keep and which he really loved. He knew he could easily let go of some of his clothes, because he was not attached to them, but he also knew he didn't want to give up his art materials and instruments because painting and playing music fed his soul. He is currently trying to make a living as an artist and is much happier than during his dark time. Although his living situation is not ideal, and money is tight, he is doing what he loves and feels spiritually and emotionally alive.

SELLING or *donating your* belongings

If you keep tripping over piles of garbage bags full of your discarded belongings because you have kept them rather than moving them on as you have gone along, there are several ways you can sell or donate your belongings. Clothes are ideal to sell to regular secondhand, or secondhand designer, stores or through an online auction site. Thrift (charity) stores are usually grateful for any good-quality clothes, if you want to donate them. Jewelry, especially gold jewelry, is another popular item to sell. Many jewelry stores buy secondhand items, particularly rings, so it is worth checking prices with a few before you sell. Several online gold stores buy gold jewelry, even if it is broken,

paying you by the carat and the weight of the pieces. Secondhand stores, such as Cash Converter, will buy electrical or electronic goods, particularly laptops, photographic equipment, and cell phones. They are also interested in sports equipment and musical instruments. In the US there are online companies that buy sports equipment that is in good condition. Several online stores will buy your old cell phone—you just have to key in the model number and they will give you a price.

If these outlets don't work for you, consider taking a pitch at a car boot sale or have a garage or yard sale, but bear in mind you have to price things quite low to

attract the customers. Advertising in local papers, which may be free for small items, can also prove successful. Specialist clubs, sports clubs, youth clubs, and local schools will often welcome donations of equipment as long as it is in good condition. Visit them to ask if they are interested in what you want to donate. Otherwise, there are websites that will recycle pieces for you.

Don't feel sad at the loss of some of the things you owned. Use the cash you have made from selling them to take a trip, do something you have always wanted to do, meet friends for a meal, or treat your family to the theater or to a movie. Remember, too, that by donating some of your possessions to clubs or thrift (charity) stores, they will go to other people who will use them and love them.

Selling

CLOTHES

Many secondhand clothes stores exist worldwide; a few are detailed here. Customers selling clothes or accessories are often paid after the item is sold. Shops normally take goods on a sale or return basis and pay commission of around 50 percent of the agreed price.

Buffalo Exchange
www.buffaloexchange.com
US company selling and trading clothes and accessories. Check website for your local store.

Cinderella's Dress Agency
www.cinderellasdressagency.co.uk
52a Shaw Road, Stockport
SK4 4AL. 0161 432 3496
Buys and sells high-street and designer wear.

Designs
www.designs-on-her.co.uk
60 Rosslyn Hill, Belsize Park,
London NW3 1ND.

020 7435 0100
Buys and sells secondhand designer clothes.

The Changing Room
www.thechangingroombrighton.co.uk
146 Islingword Road, Brighton,
BN2 9SH. 01273 622000
Buys good-quality clothes, bags, shoes, and accessories for women and children.

Clothes Agency
www.clothesagency.com
An online agency that helps to sell secondhand clothes and accessories across the internet and around the world. You have to be a member, and terms and conditions apply. Secondhand stores where clothes can be dropped off are also listed.

The Dresser
www.dresseronline.co.uk
10 Porchester Place, Connaught Village, London W2 2BS.
020 7724 7212
Higher-end designer clothes agency, specializing in the buying

and selling of contemporary and couture secondhand designer women's and menswear. They take items on a sale or return basis, and charge a 50 percent commission.

MUSICAL INSTRUMENTS
www.whybuynew.co.uk
This online store buys secondhand musical instruments. Agree on the price quoted, pack your item carefully, and arrange safe transport, or they will pick up by courier for a fee. Once the instrument is received and inspected, they will arrange payment via BACS transfer. They will also buy computers, laptops, cell phones, and MP3 players.

CDs, DVDs, AND GAMES
www.musicmagpie.co.uk
Just fill in the barcode of CDs, DVDs, or games to get an immediate price. Using the freepost service, you can download and print labels. Attach these to a box and drop off at your local post office. If sending over 50 items, you

can use their courier service for a home pick-up. Payment is by check (cheque), e-voucher or charitable donation on receipt of goods.

PHOTOGRAPHIC EQUIPMENT
www.mpbphotographic.co.uk
This site will purchase Canon and Nikon professional digital SLR photographic equipment as well as digital accessories from other manufacturers. They also purchase compact system cameras and lenses from Panasonic, Olympus, and Sony. Fill in a form for a quotation. Cameras can be posted or picked up by courier. Payment, once cameras are checked, is by BACS system.

www.realcamera.co.uk
Sevendale House, 5–7 Dale Street, Manchester M1 1JA.
0161 907 3236
Buys used photographic equipment for reasonable prices. Call or visit the store for a quotation.

JEWELRY
www.cashforyourgold.co.uk
01902 623253
Check prices online for the weight of your gold jewelry. Then request an envelope and send off via Royal Mail special delivery. Payment is by cash or check (cheque).

www.gold2pounds.com
0800 3213003
Check prices online for the weight

of your jewelry. Then request an insured freepost envelope and send your unwanted gold, silver, or platinum. Payment is by check (cheque) or money transfer.

www.postgoldforcash.com
0871 7168805
Check prices online for the weight of your gold jewelry. Then request a free gold-selling pack, list the gold, and send it in the envelope provided. Payment is by cash, bank transfer, or check (cheque).

www.gotgoldgetcash.co.uk
01642 579957
Check prices online for the weight

of your gold jewelry. Then apply for the free pack and send in your unwanted items. You will be contacted with an offer price. Payment is by check (cheque) or bank transfer.

www.sellusjewelry.com
US site buying jewelry, watches, diamonds, and gold. Call 1-800-341-3560 to find out more.

CELL PHONES
www.envirofone.com
Check the price, and then provide your details. A padded envelope and freepost address label will be sent to you to post the phone back.

Once the phone is tested and validated, you'll be sent an email confirming payment date.

www.mazumamobile.com
Search for your phone model online in the UK to get a price. Register your details, and a freepost bag will be sent to you. Post off your phone, and a check (cheque) will be sent to you upon receipt.

www.mobilephoneexchange.co.uk
Check for your phone model online in the UK to get a price. Enter your details to get a freepost, padded envelope within 48 hours. Post off the phone and once it has been checked to see if it is in working order, payment will be made by BACS within 72 hours, or by check (cheque) within seven days.

www.sellyourcell.com
Check your cell phone model on this US site to get a quote.

SPORTING EQUIPMENT
www.playitagainsports.com
Call you nearest Playitagain sports store in the US to find out the most asked-for items. Make sure your items are clean, in good condition, and include all necessary parts. Bring them to your local store for trade and payment on the spot.

ONLINE AUCTION STORES
www.ebay.co.uk
This is still the main international online auction site, where you can sell anything. Before you put up your items for sale, research similar goods already offered on the site for a description and price

comparison. You have to include a digital photo of your item, and remember to include all post and packing in the cost. Follow instructions to create a seller's account, invoice your buyer, and once payment is received, send off the goods.

SECONDHAND STORES
www.cashgenerator.co.uk
Check online for your local store in the UK. Cash Generator will buy secondhand musical instruments and sports and electronic equipment. The most wanted items are laptops, cell phones, cameras, musical instruments, and games consoles. You get paid in cash from an agreed valuation.

CAR BOOT SALES
These happen regularly throughout the UK and the US and are normally advertised by flyers or in local newspapers. Do your research on e-bay to get an idea of price for any items of value. You generally have to arrive quite early in the morning to get a good pitch. Make sure all your items are clean and in good condition. Put similar pieces together and decide on your prices. Label each item with a clear price tag—most people are seeking bargains. Display everything on tables. Display the most saleable items where they can be seen best and picked up by potential buyers. Junk and toys can be laid out on a

sheet on the ground. Clothes are a big seller, so display them well on a clothes rail. Take plenty of small change and have some plastic bags for customers who need them.

GARAGE/YARD/HOUSE SALES

Set a date and time for the sale and advertise in a local newspaper. State clearly what you are selling. For clothes and footwear, specify sizes and capitalize on the season. Popular items include sports cards, lawn mowers, camping articles, old books, jewelry, toys, and furniture. Set up tables to display the merchandise and price everything. If you live in a block, you may want to get together with some of your neighbors to hold a sale.

Donating

THRIFT OR CHARITY STORES

www.thethriftshopper.com
In the US, look at this website to find details of your local store.

Cancer Research UK
www.supportus.cancerresearchuk.org
Oxfam
www.oxfam.org.uk
British Heart Foundation
www.bhf.org.uk/shop
Barnardo's
www.barnardos.org.uk/shop
Marie Curie Cancer Care
www.mariecurie.org.uk

British Red Cross
www.redcross.org.uk
Housing Works
www.housingworks.org
Deseret Industries
www.deseretindustries.ids.org
Goodwill
www.goodwill.org
Salvation Army
www.donate.salvationarmyusa.org
www.salvationarmy.org.uk

In the UK, many high-street charity stores will take secondhand items. You can find your nearest store online. Websites for a few of the main charities in the UK and US are listed above. Most shops will accept good-quality, clean clothing, shoes and boots, jewelry, bags, and

accessories. When you have worked through the household section of this book, bear in mind they also accept books, CDs, DVDs, vinyl, musical instruments, homewares, soft furnishings, toys and games, stamps, and coins. They may not accept electronic equipment. Furniture can normally be picked up by arrangement.

www.freecycle.org
This international organization matches people who have things to give away with people who can use them. The idea is to re-use as much as possible, and keep items out of overloaded landfills. Check online for your local group. All groups are run by volunteers, and the membership is free.

PART 3

Clearing out
the home

Hoarding household clutter takes a lot of maintenance and creates dust! Having junk all over the place has a bad effect on everyone living in your home. It slows down the energy, the chi, which is the life force of everything, creating a dull, fusty atmosphere that makes it feel like everyone is walking through treacle. By going through the rooms in your home and clearing out more of the possessions that you don't need or use any more, you will notice a lighter, brighter, happier ambience, which will permeate every family member. After your massive clear-out, you can start to enjoy the emotional and spiritual freedom that having fewer possessions to deal with brings. Notice how different you and your family feel now that you are not so consumer oriented. Take time out with family and friends to enjoy more leisurely meals and have fun pursuing new outside interests. Follow some of those wonderful dreams that may have been forgotten in the chase for material gain.

LOSE that *household* clutter

You must be feeling very pleased with yourself if you have worked your way through the 100-item challenge and have reached your goal of just 100 belongings. But don't feel you can give up yet! Now you are in the frame of mind to let go of stuff, have a look at all the other family or shared household items in all the rooms of your home. The chances are it would be good to release some of these in line with the more minimalist ideas you are adopting. To see how much clutter you have acquired, look around each room with a dispassionate eye. Check all the shelves and cabinets to decide what you want, and need, and what you feel you can lose.

The entry hall or porch are the first places that may stop you in your tracks. It is so easy just to dump things in this area. Gradually, over time, everyone gets used to the junk and just squeezes past, or steps over it, every time they come in.

You may also be surprised at what you find at the back of those units in the living room; perhaps craft projects that never got finished have been stored there, or maybe a pile of old DVDs has been pushed in there and forgotten. Books may be your problem. An extensive collection can seem great, but if you never read them and they are just gathering dust, they become superfluous to your needs. The kitchen can be another real eye-opener. You may be astonished to find a yogurt or bread-maker, which seemed such a good idea at the time, hidden at the back of a cabinet. You may have used it once and now it's just taking up space. Or you may discover that you have three sets of dinner plates but only regularly use one set. And how many mugs do you actually use?

Cluttered rooms

Bedrooms can be the worst rooms in the house. I have been amazed at how cluttered clients' bedrooms are— a lot of them are certainly not the peaceful havens they should be. Some look like that TV advertisement when a girl calls on her neighbor and every room is such a mess that she thinks he has been burgled! Look under your beds: drawers that are storing bedlinen are fine but if this area is full of old junk, you are not going to have restful sleep. Children's bedrooms today often have good storage systems to hold all the toys and games, but if these are full of discarded play things, it does not create a good, positive atmosphere. It can be hard to clear out children's bedrooms, so you will have to enlist their help, encouraging them to donate any of their unwanted or unused toys to more needy children.

Your bathroom may be a shock, too, cluttered with half-finished bottles of shampoo, conditioner, or other products that you are no longer using. They may be lingering in the bathroom cabinet or stacked around the bath. Try to picture how much better it will look when it is clutter-free.

Excess paperwork, old files, magazines, and brochures are the main problem in the home office, so make sure you have a paper shredder on hand for when you start to turn this space into a creative and inspiring retreat.

In many homes, the attic is the dumping ground, hanging over you like a black cloud, and you may well feel reluctant to venture inside it. However, take a quick look to see the extent of the clear-out needed. You may be amazed by how much stuff has ended up there.

What is defined as clutter?

Clutter is any household item, or any other possession, that you no longer like or use. It can be an unwanted present, or something that is broken and that you will never repair. As mentioned earlier in the book, emotional attachment to possessions is a human weakness. The fact that a close relative or friend has given you something makes it harder to relinquish, even if you don't really like it. But that works against you because if you hang onto too many old possessions, they will keep you stuck in the past and not allow entry to all the exciting new opportunities or events that are waiting to come in. Your home is supposed to mirror you, so if it is cluttered and messy, you will be running your life in a very disorganized way.

Assessing your clutter

Now that you have looked at the scale of the task, you need to make a more detailed assessment in order to decide which cluttered areas to start clearing out first. Take a large writing pad and pen and go around each room, noting down where the main piles of junk are located. Mark whether they are in a unit, in a closet, on shelves, or just piled on the floor, and whether big or small. Use a highlighter pen to mark the piles and the room that irritate you the most, and make a start there. Have plenty of heavy-duty black trash bags ready for all the items you no longer need.

Remember, it can be very emotional letting go of possessions you have had for years, so take it slowly, working on a room for a few hours at a time. If you find yourself getting upset, take a rest, and go back to it on another day.

HOW *clutter* affects your home

In the ancient Chinese art of feng shui, good energy (chi) flow through the home is essential for harmonious living. Chi is the invisible, subtle electromagnetic energy that flows everywhere, and within everything, bringing life force with it. In the West, there are no specific words relating to chi. We tend to use words such as "mood," "atmosphere," or "spirit" of a room or home to describe our feelings when we sense it. As a feng shui consultant, my aim is to manipulate and balance this energy to create a bright and uplifting feel in the home.

Chi enters through the front door and moves in a circular, snakelike fashion through the home, exiting through the back door or windows, where more chi enters and leaves through the front door. Chi needs a positive passage through the home, so if it encounters any piles of clutter or other blockages, it slows down, making it sluggish and lethargic.

One of the worst places to have piles of clutter is in your entry hall or by the front door. This is because you are blocking the "mouth" of the home where chi first enters. If chi meets clutter here, and elsewhere, it struggles to move around the home, which can be detrimental to the family or people living there. People can feel confused, indecisive, or just stuck in a rut. When you surround yourself with possessions that you love and use on a regular basis, they give out a positive, vibrant energy that encourages normal chi flow and produces an atmosphere that makes you feel happy and content. Loved, wanted, and used items support and nurture you through invisible connecting strands. But if your home is full of unwanted junk or broken items, their negative vibes will only pull you down. The problem, too, is that the longer the junk stays around, the worse its effects on you will be. By getting rid of unwanted possessions, you will lighten your load and immediately feel better mentally, physically, and spiritually.

Clutter Blackspots

There are several major areas in the home where clutter can gather and affect how you are living, and your progress in life:

Entry hall and porch
If this area is crowded with children's paraphernalia, shoes, bags, boxes, flyers, umbrellas, and newspapers, the chi can get blocked. This can result in life becoming a struggle, with some new opportunities and prospects barred.

Understairs cupboard
It is very easy to overload this space with old sports equipment, boxes of junk, tools, electrical appliances, or old cans of paint. This in turn creates a stagnant atmosphere that will filter up to the next floor where you sleep, making life seem like hard work.

Desk
If your home-office desk is full of paperwork, old files, reports, unused reference books, magazines, and Post-it notes, it can encourage confusion, making you feel out of control.

Attic
Unfortunately, these are often the dumping grounds for our past. Too many mementoes from childhood are stored here. Broken or disused furniture, electrical items, old toys, or other unwanted pieces end up here, too, making you feel over-burdened.

Bathroom
If you have half-finished beauty or bathing products stacked around the bath and are not likely to use them up, and units full of old medical supplies and unused samples, this private retreat will make you feel restless and unsettled.

IS general or *family clutter* taking over your life?

This questionnaire will help you realize where you have a problem with household clutter, now that you have got to grips with your personal possessions. Score 2 points for a "Yes," 1 for a "Sometimes," and zero for a "No."

	Yes	Sometimes	No
GENERAL			
1 Are you upset by the household clutter in your home but can't seem to make a start on getting rid of it?			
2 Is your home full of inherited furniture that you don't really like?			
3 Have you got unwanted electrical items or gadgets that you just don't use?			
4 Does a family member have problems throwing things away?			
5 Is your garage full of junk because there is no room in the attic?			
6 Do you still have boxes from your last move that have never been opened?			
ENTRY HALL			
7 Is this full of old umbrellas, junk mail, discarded shoes, magazines, and newspapers that never get recycled?			

	Yes	Sometimes	No
KITCHEN			
8 Have you got appliances hidden away that are never used?			
9 Are there several sets of china in your cabinets, but just one that you use regularly?			
10 Do you have double the amount of mugs ever used?			
LIVING ROOM			
11 Are there racks full of DVDs, CDs, and games but you play just a few of them?			
12 Do you have stacks of candles that you never seem to get around to using?			
BEDROOM			
13 Do you tend to store all your discarded or broken items under the bed?			
14 Have you placed boxes of things you don't use on top of the wardrobe just to get them out of the way?			

	Yes	Sometimes	No
CHILDREN'S BEDROOM			
15 Are computer games and gadgets that your children have discarded stored here?			
16 Are ballet, karate, judo, or other outfits that your children don't wear any more kept here?			
17 Have your children grown out of toys but they are still stacked in boxes?			
BATHROOM			
18 Is your bathroom overstocked with beauty or bath products that will never be used?			
19 Are frayed and torn towels stacked in your bathroom cabinet?			
HOME OFFICE			
20 Do some of your files contain bank or credit card statements that are more than five years old?			
21 Have you old computers, printers, or other equipment stacked in a corner?			
22 Are your filing cabinets bulging with papers not cleared out in the last year?			

	Yes	Sometimes	No
ATTIC			
23 Do you actually know what you have stored in your attic?			
24 Can you easily get into your attic and is everything tidily stored and labeled?			
25 Do you almost have enough goods in the attic to set up a new home?			

TOTAL

THE RESULTS

40–50
You have a problem with household clutter and it is depleting your energy levels, so now is the time to start to let go. Work through the rooms one at a time, taking the advice on the following pages, clearing out what is no longer wanted or needed.

You are on your journey to a junk-free life.

30–40
Household clutter is building up in your home and detrimentally affecting the moods of everyone living there. Go through your home gradually, clearing out superfluous items, and see how good it makes you feel.

20–30
Clutter is starting to appear in your home, so get to grips with it now, removing what is not needed, and see how the overall atmosphere improves.

Below 20
Clutter is not an issue for you, but keep a close eye on what you buy. Ask yourself, "Do I need it? Is it really useful to my life?"

DOORWAY AND ENTRY *hall*

This is one of the most important parts of the home to keep clutter-free because in feng shui terms it is the "mouth" of the home where chi first enters, which makes it important to keep the area as vibrant and clean and tidy as possible. The doorway and hall should be bright and welcoming to all your visitors. If they can hardly get through the door because of all the junk that has accumulated behind it, they will feel irritated right from the start of their visit. An overcrowded hall will get you down as well. If you constantly have to climb over a mountain of

stuff just to get to the kitchen, you will feel exhausted before you even make the coffee you have been longing for. Before you start your clearout, try to envision your ideal, streamlined, clutter-free hall. Really think how you would like it to be: Do you see it newly painted with a useful storage cabinet or maybe a table with drawers? Or perhaps you see it with polished floorboards and a striking coat stand?

Getting started

Time to spend on clear-out: 2 hours

To start on your hall, get your garbage bags together, labeling one "things to sell," another "junk," and a third one "recycling." Separately label large items that won't fit in the bags. Work efficiently for the time allocated, going through the Clutter Culprits and their solutions on the right, adding any other things that you have accumulated. If this area is really cluttered and you can't get through it all in one session, allow another one to tackle what is left. This area will seem much more spacious when it's junk-free, and the atmosphere will become bright and inspiring, helping you to move on in life.

MOVING BELONGINGS ON
* Thrift (charity) stores (see page 87).
* Car boot or garage sales (see page 86).
* Local newspapers (see page 87).
* Online auction sites, such as E-bay (see page 86).

Clutter Culprits

All manner of items gather in hallways. Use these solutions to sort them out.

Problem: piles of shoes, boots, sneakers, bags
Solution: dispose of worn-out shoes or bags. Install a slim-line, pull-out unit that can hold several pairs of shoes. Make sure everyone takes their workbags to their rooms.

Problem: junk mail, flyers, leaflets, old bills, unopened credit card bills and charity collection envelopes, take-out menus, taxi or tradespeople cards, old newspapers, old keys
Solution: recycle unwanted leaflets and paper. Pay outstanding bills and file the rest. Keep wanted menus and cards in a file with plastic inserts. Dispose of old, unused keys.

Problem: bicycles, strollers, golf clubs, rackets, discarded sports gear
Solution: sell anything that is not used any more. Store bicycles, strollers and sports equipment outdoors or, if appropriate, on wall-mounted brackets or under the stairs.

Problem: home repair (DIY) materials, old tools, paints, and other paraphernalia under the stairs
Solution: safely dispose of any old tools, paints, glue, or fillers. Put up shelving or hooks to store wanted equipment.

LOVE IT, use it, or lose it

LIVING *room*

This is your room for relaxation. It is often the focal point of the home, and a place where you can recover and unwind with your family or friends after a hard day's work. Multifunctional living often exists here: there may be a space for dining and also a corner for a home office, from which the household is run efficiently. The essence of this room is tranquility and calm, but it is also a sociable room where people sit when they visit for a chat and a drink or join you for dinner. It is the place where old friends stay long into the night, discussing every subject under the sun. Having a good furniture layout with sofas and chairs grouped around a central coffee table encourages people to relax, enjoying each other's company and the conviviality. But if this room is full of clutter and too much furniture, it gives off a restless and disturbing atmosphere, making everyone feel reluctant to linger for long in the space. No one wants to be constantly tripping over piles of magazines, CDs, DVDs, discarded bags, or old craft projects; it just makes you feel frustrated and annoyed in what should be a calm, pleasant room.

Bearing in mind your mission to live with fewer possessions, picture in your head the ideal layout for your junk-free living space. Do you see it with good storage units and nothing stacked on the floor? Maybe you visualize it with less furniture and the shelves cleared of some of your accessories and books for a cleaner, tidier look? Perhaps you see yourself throwing out your two old sofas and replacing them with a big corner sofa?

Clutter Culprits

Follow these solutions to achieve some order once more in this room.

Problem: overloaded bookshelves
Solution: keep the books you love and take all those unwanted ones to a thrift (charity) store, or donate them to a hospital or school library.

Problem: old CVDs, DVDs, games
Solution: sort out the ones that are not played any more and sell them on through specialist or secondhand stores, or online. Alternatively, take them to a thrift (charity) store.

Problem: old magazines
Solution: cut out any articles of interest to keep for reference and file in a plastic-sleeved folder, and recycle the rest.

Problem: too many accessories
Solution: if you are fed up with a lot of the *objets* on your shelves, decide which ones you still love and take the rest to a thrift (charity) store, or sell them at a car boot or garage sale.

Problem: damaged or broken furniture
Solution: take to the dump any pieces that cannot be repaired or you don't like any more. Alternatively, arrange a collection from a thrift (charity) store. If you still want to keep the piece, have it repaired by professionals.

Problem: inherited items, such as relatives' knickknacks, clocks, pictures, ceramic collections
Solution: keep only what you really love and items that will always remind you of the person who owned them originally. Dispose of any mementoes that are worthless, and sell good clocks, pictures, or collections at auction or to an antique store.

Problem: loose photographs and old albums
Solution: go through these when you are feeling strong—photographs can make you very emotional. Throw out unwanted shots or pictures of people you can't remember, no longer see, or dislike. Think about storing photos in index systems, so it's easy to leaf through them. Look through your old albums and try to refine them—if you have eight, for example, try to cut them down to four, including the pictures you love.

Getting started

Time to spend on clear-out: 4 hours

Collect some garbage bags. Label the first bag "things
to sell," the next one "junk," and the third one "friends
or thrift/charity." Put labels on large items. Sort
steadily through the Clutter Culprits on the left, plus
anything else that may not be included on the list. If
your living room is really overloaded and you can't get
through it all in one session, allow time for another
one. Once you have cleared out all the unwanted
items, your living room will start to breathe again, and
you will love its positive, vibrant atmosphere, which
will make you want to invite friends over.

MOVING BELONGINGS ON

* Thrift (charity) stores (see page 87).
* Specialist and online stores for CDs, DVDs, and games
  (see page 84).
* Car boot or garage sales (see page 86).
* Auctions or antique stores.
* Local newspapers (see page 84).
* Hospital or school libraries.

LOVE IT,
use it, or
lose it

Mary's Blog

I'm rushing to write this, because I'm going out to
dinner tonight. At least I can easily find what I want
to wear in my pared-down wardrobe. Do I miss
what's gone? I don't think so—I am virtually down to
my 100 items, so that's good. What is really tough is
not browsing around the stores as much as I used to,
because I know I may be tempted to buy something
I don't desperately need. I avoided the sales like the
plague but okay, "hands-up," I did buy some much-
needed pantyhose and socks but, honestly, they were
replacing ones that have worn out.

   Moving on... I ventured into the kitchen the other
day with my de-cluttering hat on. I didn't think I was
that bad with household items but I have lived in
this house for nearly five years now and several
things have still not seen the light of day. What do
you think? Do you keep baking equipment you only
use once or twice a year? I don't know about you but
some dishes I use all the time and others just seem
to sit there. I kept a set of cups for visitors but have
only used mugs since I moved. And 27 cookbooks!
How did I end up with so many? And I have used
just a few recipes from each one—okay, I can feel a
purge coming on.

KITCHEN

A warm and nurturing environment, the kitchen is often thought of as the "heart" of the home. Family and friends love to gather here to chat and catch up on all the news, and they often eat here, if it is a large, open space. Everyone who visits loves to feel embraced by its cheering ambience, and have their appetites stimulated by wonderful, sensuous cooking smells. Kids often linger, doing their homework, while adults will take some time out of their busy schedules to read a newspaper or book in this comforting, cosseting place. The ideal kitchen has clear, tidy countertops, adequate storage, and ordered cabinets, making this room an uplifting place to be. However, countertops are often cluttered with every gadget imaginable, cabinets are overflowing with china and kitchen products, and fridges and freezers contain food that will never get eaten. This overcrowding can upset the balance and harmony needed here. Friends and family will get fed up searching for that buried egg whisk or trying to find that packet of white sauce in a cabinet—somewhere.

Before you get to grips with de-junking your kitchen and having a simpler lifestyle, think what your ideal kitchen would be like. Do you see tidy cabinets with some pull-out baskets and products neatly ordered? Have you a vision of gleaming, clear countertops and a floor with nothing stacked on it?

Clutter Culprits

Take note of these solutions to achieve a workable streamlined space.

Problem: unused or broken china, duplicate dinner or tea sets, old mugs and casserole dishes
Solution: throw out broken china. Take unwanted dishes, mugs, and dinner or tea sets to a thrift (charity) store, or sell online or through a local newspaper.

Problem: unwanted gadgets, such as yogurt or ice-cream makers and juicers
Solution: if these are working and in good condition, sell them online or through a local newspaper. Alternatively, give them to friends.

Problem: too many packaged kitchen products, sauces, cans, oils, and spices
Solution: throw out what's stale (check "use by" dates); give away what's not needed. Store similar items together. Use baskets to create some tidy storage in cabinets.

Problem: decaying cleaning products and materials
Solution: throw out old cleaning liquids (dispose of them responsibly) and cleaning cloths; keep only what you use regularly, and store in pull-out baskets. Give away any unwanted, impulse buys that you find.

LOVE IT, use it, or *lose it*

Getting started

Time to spend on clear-out: 3 hours

Collect your garbage bags. Label one "things to sell" (use a box for big gadgets), label the second "junk," and the third "friends or thrift (charity) store." Go through the Cutter Culprits list on the left, adding anything else you may have. Schedule in another session if you need more time. Cleared cabinets and countertops will make preparation and cooking a pleasure again, and the uplifting atmosphere will attract people like a magnet.

MOVING BELONGS ON
* Thrift (charity) stores (see page 87).
* Online auction sites, such as E-bay (see page 86).
* Local newspapers (see page 84).

BEDROOM

Your bedroom is your personal sanctuary, a place where you can close the door behind you and escape work or home worries. Winding down in bed, you can calm your mind, emotions, and spirit in this soothing, peaceful space. You can also escape here for a nap after a tiring day or to grab some time just for yourself, to read on your own. Since this is a place where your body re-generates itself and your spirit rests, you want to be soothed and pampered by the atmosphere. The clean lines of a comfortable bed with coordinated bedding positioned opposite the door, balanced by bedside cabinets and lamps, a tidy wardrobe or closet, and a dressing table, will make you sigh with pleasure as you enter the room. Boxes toppling off the top of the wardrobe, clothes dumped on the floor, an overflowing laundry hamper, and junk thrown under the bed will generate a completely opposite response: your heart will sink every time you enter this untidy, muddled room.

A clutter-free bedroom is essential for good sleep, and should be a priority in your quest for a simpler life. How do you want this room to be? Do you see a

Use the solutions to tidy up the room.

Problem: boxes of junk on top of the wardrobes
Solution: these will give you a headache, because you will think they are going to fall on you so sort through the boxes and throw out what's not needed. Store the remainder in pull-out boxes or baskets inside cabinets.

Problem: a pile of broken hairdryers, old shoes, old bedlinen, discarded T-shirts under the bed
Solution: safely dispose of the hairdryers and other broken electrical equipment. Throw out old shoes, bedlinen, and T-shirts. Any in good condition, take to a thrift (charity) store. For more storage, have drawers under the bed but only store clean, untorn bedlinen or extra clothes here.

LOVE IT, use it, or *lose it*

room painted in pleasant pastel colors with a cozy bed, complementary bedlinen, and big, plumped-up pillows? Perhaps you want a more feminine look with frilly drapes and lacy bed coverings, or maybe you would like the bed to be tented? Alternatively, a more modern room with contrasting, neutral color shades may be the style you want?

Getting started

Time to spend on clear-out: 2–3 hours

Collect your garbage bags. Label the first "junk," the second "friends or thrift (charity) store." Work positively through the Clutter Culprits list on the right, adding anything extra you have stashed here. If you find yourself battling to get everything done in the time specified, just allocate time for another clear-out. As the clutter disappears, you will feel a positive shift in atmosphere. The "fug" will lift and your bedroom will be a safe haven once more.

MOVING BELONGINGS ON

Some of the ways to dispose of items from your bedroom are covered on pages 64–66 and 70–71. Move on what's left by taking it to a thrift (charity) store (see page 87).

Child's BEDROOM

Many children consider their bedrooms to be their special place, where they can hide from the world, play games, read, make up wonderful stories, work on their computer, listen to music, and entertain their friends. It can often be a dual-purpose room with a quiet area for relaxing and sleeping and another, more stimulating space for playing and studying. An ordered desk, a comfy bed with colorful bedlinen, and toys stored away in stacking boxes will make your child feel safe and secure. But, as we know, children can be notoriously untidy, and will often leave toys, books, and clothes scattered around the room. Their work or play area can be a disaster of discarded cars, dolls, electronic games, computer games, old paintings, and schoolwork. All this confusion can make the energy restless here, disturbing children's schoolwork and upsetting their sleep.

Before you start working on your child's bedroom clutter, try to visualize this room when it is de-junked. Are you encouraging your child to follow your simple living ethos? Do you see a desk in the corner with shelves above it stacked with loved books, disks, and games? Do you imagine the bed with a supportive headboard and soft lamps on tables either side of the bed? Have all the remaining toys and games miraculously been stored in big colorful drawers or in stacking boxes? Perhaps soft toys, if your child is young, are now hanging in canvas hanging racks with numerous pockets?

Clutter Culprits

Use the solutions to restore order.

Problem: piles of toys and games
Solution: throw away anything that is broken. Give toys in good condition to thrift (charity) stores or hospitals, or to sales held to raise money for your child's school.

Problem: too many computer and electronic games, old CDs and DVDs
Solution: give to friends, sell via online sites, such as E-bay, or to secondhand stores, or donate to sales for your child's school.

Problems: stacks of books
Solution: keep the well-loved favorites and give away the rest.

Problem: unwanted or outgrown clothes
Solution: check what clothes your child likes to wear and pass on unwanted or outgrown items to children of friends or hold an exchange party. Alternatively, take them to a thrift (charity) store.

LOVE IT, use it, or lose it

Getting started

Time to spend on clear-out: 2 hours

Work on this room together with your child. Collect your garbage bags. Label one "junk," another "toys to sell," and a third "thrift (charity) store." Label a large box for bigger toys, or just label them separately. Go through the Clutter Culprits list on the left and if the room is too overloaded to get through it all in one session, just book in another one. After a few arguments, your child will sigh with relief as his/her special room emerges from its clutter, making him/her feel nurtured and happy once more.

MOVING BELONGINGS ON
* Thrift (charity) stores (see page 87).
* Secondhand stores and online sites for CDs, DVDs, computer and electronic games (see page 84).
* Either donate directly to hospitals, clubs, or local schools, or to sales held to raise money for these good charitable causes.

BATHROOM

Sinking into a hot, fragrant bath is one of life's pleasures. Relaxing in the calming water, you can wash away any negativity from the day and forget your problems, cleansing your mind, body, and soul. Here you can escape from the demands of your family and the outside world, and have some time for contemplation or meditation. What you need in this space is a warm and appealing atmosphere; it should be a place to linger, where you will feel cherished. Being surrounded by fluffy towels and mats, calming pictures, and tidy storage cabinets and hanging units can make you feel that you are in your own unique retreat. Surfaces packed full of half-finished bathing and beauty products, too many units or baskets, and fraying or torn towels bring out exactly the opposite response: you just feel restless, dissatisfied, and unsettled in this messy room.

An inviting, organized bathroom will help you chill and take time out, and is a must for the "life with less" that you are seeking. But how do you see the refuge of your dreams? Has it got cabinets with tidily stacked products, or maybe units with pull-out drawers so that you can find things easily? Maybe your ideal is a freestanding unit with open shelves so that you can store your towels? Is the bath cleared of all clogged-up products and surrounded by candles?

Clutter Culprits

Use the following solutions to bring some order to the bathroom.

Problem: full medicine cabinet
Solution: throw away out-of-date creams, plasters, and ointments. Return antibiotics or other strong pills to the pharmacy to be disposed of responsibly.

Problem: too many bath oils, shampoos, conditioners, and other beauty products, often half-finished
Solution: throw away opened products that you will never use again and that are cluttering up the bath and shower. Give away any that are unopened. Hang up a new cabinet or buy a unit, if necessary, and store what you want to keep, tidily, so you can find what you need.

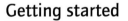

LOVE IT, use it, or *lose it*

Problem: old towels and mats, and units cluttering up the bathroom
Solution: dispose of torn, worn, or stained towels and mats—they just pull down the energy here. Store the ones you've kept by color in a unit. Sell any unwanted units locally.

Getting started

Time to spend on clear-out: 1½–2 hours

Collect your garbage bags. Label the first one "junk." If you have pieces of furniture to dispose of, just put a label on them. Label a second bag "friends or thrift (charity) store." Make sure you go through the Clutter Culprits list above, adding anything not included there. Two hours should be enough time but add on a bit more if you are still not finished. Once this room is cleared of all the garbage, notice how "light" and inviting it seems once more.

MOVING BELONGINGS ON
* Thrift (charity) stores (see page 87).
* Local newspapers (see page 84).

HOME *office*

A creative and inspiring environment, this is where you spend time paying bills, juggling the household budget, and possibly doing your own freelance work. Clarity and concentration are important here in order for you to make the right decisions. If you are doing your own work in this space, it is here that you promote yourself to the world, showing your talent for bringing wealth, prosperity, and success into your life. For you to achieve this, the room should be pleasant, well lit, and organized, with all the equipment you need at your fingertips. However, your creativity and positive attitude will slide if your desk is covered with paperwork, bills, Post-its, pens, and crumpled stationery. If you are surrounded by gadgets that no longer work, and filing cabinets that you can hardly open, your heart will sink every time you enter this workroom.

An ordered office will boost your business skills, and help you plan how to spend less money in your simplified lifestyle. So how do you see this productive area working? Do you see a bright room with an attractive wooden filing cabinet, tidy desk, and stacking filing trays for all your bills and correspondence? Or if your office is in your living room, does it contain an ingenious unit that folds away but contains slimline drawers and a sliding flap for typing on your laptop?

Getting started

Time to spend on clear-out: 2 hours

Collect some trash bags. Label the first one "recycling," the second "junk," and a third "thrift (charity) store." If you have equipment or furniture to dispose of, label it separately. Follow your Clutter Culprits list on the right, including anything else that is not listed there. If your office is packed to the gunwales with paperwork or old equipment, schedule in some more time to finish clearing out. When order is restored to this creative room, and the "mustiness" and untidiness disappear, you will notice how inspired and mentally alert you feel sitting at your desk.

Clutter Culprits

Use these solutions to take control of this creative space once more.

Problem: messy desk
Solution: shred any old correspondence that's not needed. File any bills or important letters. Transfer numbers, notes, or addresses on Post-its to your phone or diary. Junk any old stationery, leaking pens, or broken pencils.

Problem: packed filing cabinet
Solution: sort through your files, recycling where possible and shredding anything else that is redundant until you have a neat, workable, and current cabinet.

Problem: old furniture, broken or unused electrical equipment
Solution: remove unwanted furniture and donate to a thrift (charity) store if appropriate (arrange collection for large pieces). Dump broken equipment at your local refuse facility, sell unused pieces online or at a secondhand store.

LOVE IT, use it, or lose it

MOVING BELONGINGS ON

* Thrift (charity) stores (see page 87).

* Online auction sites, such as E-bay (see page 86).

* Second-hand stores, (see page 86).

ATTIC

How do you view your attic? Do you see it as a space to dump unused things, or to store relics from your past? The attic all too often becomes a junkyard for our memories, stockpiling inherited items that no one wants, old school trophies and awards, discarded toys, romantic memorabilia, and unwanted sports equipment. Your home's past seems to linger here, hanging over your family and friends like a murky, dark cloud. Unwanted gifts can be abandoned into this dark space, leaving a feeling of negativity and disapproval. An attic can be a perfect, well-lit space, with good storage units, where you can keep rarely used possessions. But if you can hardly get into it because of the boxes packed to the roof, or the mass of junk that has been dumped there, you will feel chained to your past and scared of moving forward.

A tidy, well-organized, and junk-free attic will take you well on your path to living with less. But what does your ideal attic space look like? Has it got good shelving, clearly labeled boxes, hanging rails for sports clothes, and units for tools? Do you see it brightly lit with everything neatly sorted on racks?

Clutter Culprits

Follow the solutions to reclaim your storage space.

Problem: old equipment, such as exercise bikes, golf clubs, old skis, rackets, and mini trampolines
Solution: throw out any decrepit equipment, sell anything in good condition online or to a secondhand store, or give it to a good cause.

Problem: memorabilia, such as old schoolbooks, college and school projects, diplomas or degrees, love letters
Solution: keep diplomas, have a special "memories" box for a few love letters and treasured items, and ditch the rest.

Problem: old games and playing cards, old toys
Solution: keep any games and playing cards that you will play again regularly and give away the rest.

Problem: old decorating materials
Solution: throw out opened paints, stains, or varnishes that are no longer usable, dried-up brushes, and old rags. Keep recently used paint (for touching up), and cleaned brushes, rollers, and trays in a labeled plastic storage container.

LOVE IT, use it, or *lose it*

Getting started

Time to spend on clear-out: 3-4 hours

Collect some garbage bags. Label the first one "junk" (you may need several), the second "recycling," the third "thrift (charity) store," and the fourth "things to sell." Go through your Clutter Culprits list on the left, adding any items not detailed there. A packed attic may take more than four hours to sort out, so book another session. Clearing out old junk from your past and tidying up the attic will bring a huge shift in energy. The heavy "cloud" above you will lift, and you will find the impetus to move forward once again.

MOVING BELONGINGS ON
* Online auction sites, such as E-bay (see page 86).
* Secondhand stores, (see page 86).
* Thrift (charity) stores (see page 87).
* Sales for good causes.

BACK *yard (garden)*

This is your retreat from the world, a place where you can relax and sunbathe or read a book on a summer's afternoon. It is here that you grow beautiful, scented flowers or harvest bountiful produce for everyone to enjoy. On balmy afternoons and evenings, you can entertain your friends and family with barbecues or light, summer meals, relishing the long, daylight hours. Manicured lawns, a spotless patio or decked area, and glorious shrubs will feed your soul every time you walk into this type of garden. But if you have to pick your way over the cracked or moss-laden patio onto the overgrown lawn, being attacked by prickly bushes every step of the way, you will feel annoyed, irritated, and let down by this neglected and forgotten area.

A well-laid-out and organized garden will help keep you in the right frame of mind for a less stressful lifestyle. But how do you see your dream garden? Does it have a tidy lawn, a pergola, and a host of colorful flowers? Or do you prefer a raised patio area for eating and then a paved garden with lots of colorful pots and summer blooms?

Clutter Culprits

Use the solutions to make your back yard (garden) more appealing.

Problem: faded, broken, or unused garden furniture; ripped or stained cushions
Solution: ditch any furniture that is irreparable. Otherwise, repair broken wooden supports, restain and revarnish where appropriate, and replace fabric or cushions. Sell or give away unwanted furniture in good condition.

Problem: shed or garden building full of rusting tools, old or unused machinery, decaying barbecues, broken bicycles, and old plant fertilizers
Solution: junk any old equipment and bicycles, old plant foods, seeds, and any gadgets that are beyond repair. Sort out what machinery and tools

LOVE IT, use it, or lose it

you want to keep, and clean and oil them. Hang cleaned tools on hooks or a tool bar. Sell the rest. Add more shelves to take equipment off the floor. Store often-used chairs and barbecues by the door.

Problem: decaying, cracked, or chipped flowerpots, and pots full of weeds
Solution: throw out frost-damaged pots or any beyond repair. Clean up and re-use the others. Fill with new potting soil and grow some seasonal flowering plants to boost the energy here.

Getting started

Time to spend on clear-out: 3 hours

Use several heavy-duty garden trash bags. Add a garbage bag labeled "things to sell" and another labeled "thrift (charity) store." Work down the Clutter Culprits list above, adding any bits and pieces not included. If you find that three hours is not long enough to tame your back yard (garden), arrange time for another session. Restoring your back yard to its former glory will remove the air of decay. You will be able to smell the flowers, and be tempted to linger here, enjoying your outside space once more.

MOVING BELONGINGS ON
* Local newspapers (see page 84).
* Car boot or garage sales (see page 87).
* Thrift (charity) stores (see page 87).

PART 4

Your new
minimalist life

Living a simpler life with fewer possessions in your home can be totally liberating. Releasing things you have kept for a while brings in a new, fresh energy that affects everybody. You will feel freer and less tied to having to earn money to buy more new things that you don't really need. It doesn't mean you have to live frugally but that you become mindful about your money, and live within your means. The money you have saved by not buying so many things can fund those hobbies you never had time for, go toward a new creative course, or just be used for fun days out or catching up with friends. Now that you are not in pursuit of material gain, you can take time to set some more spiritual goals. What is it that your inner self, your heart, really desires for the next few years? Spending time in the countryside, traveling abroad, doing voluntary work to help other people, and really connecting with those close to you will bring far more rewards than material possessions ever can.

LIVING *a simpler* lifestyle

How has getting rid of your clutter gone? Are you close to living with just 100 items? I expect it has been quite an emotional journey. Letting go of once-loved belongings is never easy, but as soon as they are gone, you can feel truly free. Do you look around your home now and feel that every painting, every accessory, and every book means something special to you? You may find that once you start releasing household items, you can't stop. Some people decide to live with very little furniture and soft furnishings; others decide they need more to achieve the level of comfort they want. Just go with what feels right for you. Becoming more of a minimalist does not mean that you can't own things. We all need a certain level of material comfort. It just means that you have stepped away from excessive consumerism on your way to a more authentic life. You can still own a car, computer, or television, but don't let yourself get brainwashed by the advertising campaigns into believing that you need to buy the latest model every year. Being more minimalist means promoting the things you value the most— decide what is really important in your life and remove those things that distract you from this.

Now you are learning to curb your excessive spending habits, don't you feel so much better and less stressed? The money you are not spending on new gadgets, clothes, or equipment for the home can be saved or used to pay off any existing debts, or to pay for hobbies or other events you didn't have time for before. Horseback riding may have been a childhood passion that has been put on the back burner until recently. You may have always wanted to spend several weeks or months traveling overseas, and now you can save for that special trip of a lifetime. Or maybe there's a course you want to take that you never managed to save for, until now. Make a resolution to do the things that you love, but live within your means from now on, and give up the life you spent living on credit.

How can I benefit from becoming a minimalist?

Removing unwanted possessions from your life and changing your attitude to consumerism and constant shopping is challenging but brings many positive rewards.

* You have more time to redefine what you want out of life.

* You can show your authentic self to the world, and take time to listen to your inner needs.

* You can stop working so hard, and take the time to form more meaningful relationships with the people you love.

* As you buy fewer things, you won't have to achieve so much at work, and can spend more free time with the important people in your life.

* Spending less time shopping will free you up to do other, creative things.

* You can appreciate the open spaces in your home. You no longer keep tripping over things, and it gives you a wonderful, free feeling.

* Your life is less stressful and more contemplative.

Your ideal life

Has it just recently dawned on you how little spare time you have? Maybe you don't want that promotion at work any more but would rather stop working overtime and have some time for yourself and your family? You may decide to change your job or even consider going part-time if you are close to retirement age. Allowing yourself some free time from "busyness," you can quieten that loud outer voice and connect with your inner whisperings about your future goals or dreams. As you build the image of your future, look around your home and see if the belongings you have left fit in with the image of your new life, or match your aspirations? Maybe you have always wanted to take up photography but have never found the time, and now you want to convert one of your bedrooms into a studio. Will you need to do some more clearing out to achieve this aim? Or perhaps you want to convert your garden shed or outbuilding into a small office so that you can simplify your life by working from home. Will you have to get rid of more tools and garden furniture that may be stored here? You may want to socialize more, and are longing to convert your garage into a spare guest room, but will you need to do a big clear-out first?

Clearing out your home allows for new thinking, and lets new opportunities present themselves. You may realize that you are ready for a more drastic change, possibly a move from the city to the country, for example. Working in an office may no longer appeal to you and you may decide to re-train as a therapist or work with animals.

Living with less

Now that you have got used to living with less, you may feel you want to take it a stage further. Do you feel you still have too much furniture? One way of cutting down on furniture in the home is to exchange some items for multifunctional pieces. If you are using your spare room as an office, for example, and don't

want a bed in there, think about having a sofa that converts into a bed in your living space. Perhaps replacing two sofas with one large one with a corner return would give you more space. Some single beds fold back into seats or side tables. Ingenious coffee tables can be converted into dining tables by adjusting the legs. Need more storage? Buy a chest that doubles up as a coffee table. To create more space in the center of your living room, buy a nest of tables, which can be stored by the wall and pulled out when needed. Some versatile shelf units have one side for books and accessories, and the other, narrower side for storing DVDs and games. If you have just got rid of some novels to the thrift (charity) store, think about buying an e-reader or join your local library.

If working in your living room is a necessity, consider a slimline desk with narrow drawers and a pull-out shelf for your laptop. Losing a storage unit in a bedroom? Units are available that slide under the bed. But only store clothes or bedlinen here, because a mix of other possessions can possibly disrupt your sleep.

When you remove excessive belongings from your life and step away from materialistic desires, it creates the opportunity for a significant life change to take place. When you get off the treadmill of a busy life, you need to stop for a moment and ask yourself, "What am I doing with my life? What will make me happy?" Think carefully about what you want out of your future, and take the necessary steps to achieve it.

Living more simply can change you forever. You slow down and stop being a slave to the consumerist lifestyle. You learn to "live in the now," appreciating every day of your wonderful existence.

Mary's Blog

I can't believe I have nearly finished writing the book—I have really been on a journey with it for the last few months. I am finding these dull winter days a bit depressing, but they do put me in the frame of mind to keep clearing out more stuff: I gave away two of my old summer baskets to a friend yesterday. I also decided that some chick-lit novels needed to go to the thrift (charity) store. I often buy them from the man on the beach, who sells a great selection, but they clutter up my shelves pretty quickly. Have I got the energy to tackle my office next? It's packed full of reference books that hardly seem to get looked at now... I have battled a bit with the challenge of living with 100 items but I have only replaced things since I started, and I have noticed a change in my shopping habits—I still lust after some pretty clothes but I make myself resist. How have you got on? I wish you well and hope you've made progress too, and will continue to enjoy living your life of less.

*A minimalist values quality,
not quantity, in all forms.*

Leo Babauta, writer

Index

Further reading

Affluenza, Oliver James, Ebury Publishing
Simple Living Guide, Janet Luhrs, Broadway
The Power of Less, Leo Babauta, Hay House
Organized Simplicity, Tsh Oxenreider, Betterway Books
Joy of Less, A Minimalist Living Guide, Francine Jay, Anja Press
The Ultimate Guide to Clearing Your Clutter, Mary Lambert, Cico Books

Picture credits

Acknowledgments

I would like to thank my managing editors, Dawn Bates and Clare Sayer, for their creative help in this project. A very special thank you goes to my sister Gill in Portugal, and to Simon, Emma, Marina, and Rafael in Italy, for all their support and encouragement when I was writing on those dark winter days. Finally, to my friends Claire M, Tim, Anna, Lucy, Liz, Claire G, Linda, Jackie, Sue, Fran, and Sarah, who dragged me away from my computer to have film nights and to go out for a few glasses of red wine and friendly conversation. Also thanks to Suzi, who always made me laugh over our fun lunches, and who gave me some useful input for my blogs.

Mary Lambert is based in Brighton and can be contacted for feng shui and decluttering consultations for homes and businesses, and for workshops, via her website: www.marylambertfengshui.com